TREVOR NOAH

Biography of the Famous South African Comedian

By: Lawrence Barnes

Table of Contents

Introduction 4

Chapter 1: Trevor's Origins 8

Chapter 2: Early Childhood Days 15

Chapter 3: Education 21

Chapter 4: A Special Relationship 30

Chapter 5: How to Look Alike and to Be Different 40

Chapter 6: Love Life 46

Chapter 7: A Booming Business 62

Chapter 8: Things are Falling Apart 77

Chapter 9: Abel 84

Closing Thoughts 87

Introduction

The region of South Africa was inhabited since prehistoric times and was a region that attracted populations from all over Africa. The Khoisan population was the indigenous population in this part of the world, but they were driven away to the arid lands by the Bantu invasion, which originated from Central West Africa (the Congo basin). Of these migrant groups, the Nguni peoples, formed by the Swazi, Ndebele, Zulu, and Xhosa tribes settled close to the eastern coast of this territory, while the Sotho-Tswana tribes (Tswana, Pedi, and Sotho peoples) chose to settle on the interior plateau, also known as the Highveld. The North-western part of modern-day South Africa was inhabited by the Tsonga, Lemba, and Venda tribes.

All these tribes were divided, and there were often conflicts between them. The first Europeans to arrive in South Africa were the Portuguese. However, their interaction with the local population was minor because they were mostly interested in discovering a trading route to the Far East. In the second half of the 17th century began the Dutch colonization, who wanted to create an enclave, a permanent settlement, on the spice route with India and the Far East. The first Dutch ships arrived on the South African coasts on April 6, 1652. VOC (Vereenigde Oostindische Compagnie) was the company responsible for the development of the settlement, so they brought over farmers and slaves to strengthen the base and to provide food supplies and shelter for the passing ships. The slaves were originally from the Dutch colonies of Indonesia, so at this point, the South African territory was populated with different races: the native black, the European whites (Dutch, German, and French) and the slaves from Indonesia. There were some conflicts between the blacks and the

Europeans, but the local tribes couldn't destroy the Dutch settlement. Inevitably, the mixture of the race was only a matter of time, so the "hybrid" babies were soon born after the Dutch settled in South Africa.

The settlement has taken more portions of land, and many other settlers came to South Africa to live in this colony. Amongst the colonists were farmers of Dutch, German, and French origins, who also brought Christianism to these lands, but it wasn't Catholicism that was present in South Africa, it was protestant religions like the Dutch Reformed Church, the Lutheran Church, and the Calvinist Church. A new language was born, Afrikaans, which was Dutch with some strong influence from the Zulu language. To this day, Afrikaans is still an official language in South Africa.

In the 19th century, just after the Napoleonic Wars, the Kingdom of Holland lost control over South Africa, and the British Empire took over the colonies, which was not something the Afrikaners (Dutch colonists, also known as the Boers) were very comfortable with. Slowly, the English influence over these colonies increased, leading to the abolishment of slavery. This caused many Dutch settlers to migrate inland and get in conflict with the local tribes. However, not only the Boers adventured inland, but also the British were very curious about what this land had to offer. This is what led to the discovery of diamonds and gold in South Africa. On many occasions, the European sides were victorious against local tribes, so they easily secured land inside this country. This is how the Boer republics were born, like the Orange Free State and the Transvaal Republic, as forms of resistance against the British. Conflict over the natural resources of the South African soil was imminent, and the Anglo-Boer Wars started. The Boers were victorious in the First Anglo-Boer War, but the British were determined to seize the control over the Witwatersrand gold mines and eventually defeated the Boers using troops from all over the British Empire. The year 1902 marked the end of the Second Anglo-Boer War and also the fall of the Transvaal Republic. In 1910, the Union of South Africa was founded—a state which united the Orange Free State, Natal, Transvaal, and Cape Colony into one country. It was a British Independent Dominion in the form of a constitutional monarchy, with the British monarch being represented by a Governor. Other territories, like modern-day Lesotho, Swaziland, and Botswana, were placed directly under British rule. The union parliament had a pro-British politics, but they also issued some very harsh segregationist laws, like the 1913 Natives' Land Act, which limited the land available for the majority black population to 8%, more than 90% of the available land was in possession of the white people, who were around 20% of the total population.

The biggest political force of the time was the South African Party, but it also had a more radical wing, with some Boers politicians who were against the pro-British political direction. This wing formed the National Party, a group which followed the Afrikaner's interests and also independence from Britain. In 1924, the National Party rose to power in coalition with the Labor Party, and since then they had a racial and nationalist view, trying to get away from British influence until they finally succeeded in 1960, when a vast majority of white South Africans voted to leave the Commonwealth and establish the Republic of South Africa. Many Afrikaners shared their political view, so this party was in power for many years to come. Some of the politicians of the National Party had Pro-German and Neo-Nazi views, which fit quite well with their agenda, as the minority white population had rights and properties, while the majority black population didn't have any rights.

Driven by Neo-Nazi beliefs, the Afrikaner National Party implemented—since 1948—the apartheid, which means separateness. This is the perfect example when the slogan "divide and conquer" is successfully put into action. Such a policy was intended to separate the white minority of South Africa from the non-white population, but also to divide the black population into tribes, to weaken their political power. It was the perfect racial segregation, as the National Party wanted to prevent any mixture between races. That's why they banned marriages between whites and other races, and also sexual relations between whites and other races. This has become a law, and any person caught breaking this law would suffer severe consequences, especially blacks. Non-white communities were separated from white communities, so they had separate development. Blacks were only entitled to work in mines or other hard jobs with low wages, and in some cases, the apartheid would separate families because any mixed child was not allowed to leave in a white community, as he/she was considered colored.

The black community rebelled against this oppressive regime, establishing military wings to fight against the authorities since they quickly realized that peaceful protests were not effective. Nelson Mandela was the leader of a military wing and was imprisoned from 1963 – 1990. He was the symbol of resistance against the apartheid.

Trevor Noah experienced all the hardship of the apartheid era, having a black mother and a white father (who was originally from Switzerland). In the chapters of this book, you will find some interesting stories from his childhood and teenage years, many of them being in the context of apartheid.

Chapter 1:
Trevor's Origins

Trevor's Mom

Trevor's mom is Patricia Nombuyiselo Noah, a wild and impulsive woman of Xhosa heritage. She was raised deeply religious, but also had an extraordinary ambition to become an independent woman. Patricia's parents were Temperance and Frances Noah, both of them black people of the Xhosa heritage. They met in Sophiatown and married, but the government seized their property, along with other properties of the black people, to build a modern white suburb called Triumph. They were relocated in Meadowlands, a neighborhood of Soweto (which is in the Johannesburg area). Frances divorced Temperance and moved to Orlando (a neighborhood in Soweto) with all her kids.

Patricia was the second child: she has a bigger sister, Sibongile, and a younger brother, Velile. As the second born, she felt unwanted, and that's why she had a rebellious, stubborn, and defiant attitude. She adored her father, Temperance, who wasn't the family type of parent. He was always chasing after women and didn't care about his family. Still, when she was nine, Patricia wanted to live with her father, but every time she spent time with him, Temperance would take her to local bars called shebeens. To her disappointment, she didn't live with her father afterward, as he sent her to the Xhosa homelands in Transkei to live with her aunt (Temperance's sister). Patricia didn't get the attention she deserved from her mother, father, or aunt, and she strived for independence. She lived in Transkei for around 14 years, spending her childhood and teenage years doing farm work, like plowing fields and herding animals. The region was scarce of water since most of the land with water and good soil was taken by the

8

white farmers. Most of the black communities had Bantu schools, which were educational institutions founded by the government, specialized in preparing black people to work. They would be prepared for working in mines, or in the fields, while women were prepared to become maids. Patricia was lucky enough to attend a Catholic school, where she learned English from a white pastor. This is how she learned to read and write in English, which at that point was considered a major advantage. Her first job was at a factory in a town nearby, where she made school uniforms on a sewing machine; but she wasn't paid in cash, she only received a plate of warm food at the end of the day. When she was 21, her aunt fell ill, and she couldn't keep her in Transkei anymore. So, she returned to Soweto, where her mother, sister, and brother lived.

The usual job for a black woman during apartheid was to work as a maid or in a factory, but she already experienced this type of work, and it was not good enough for her. Patricia was a very intelligent woman and someone who can adapt to all situations. She could fluently speak languages of the South African tribes like Xhosa, Zulu, and the official languages of the white community: Afrikaans and English. As apartheid was getting "softer," she saw an opportunity to work as a secretary, and she attended a typing course to get the necessary skills. She quickly got a job as a secretary and started earning more than anyone in the house, but she couldn't keep her salary. Since she was living in her mother's house, she had to contribute to all of the expenses. The family needed a refrigerator, an oven, and a radio; now with Patricia's salary, all of these were possible. Since she didn't have much freedom in Soweto, just like in Transkei, she ran away in the city, determined to sleep in public restrooms and depend on the kindness of prostitutes to make it in the world.

She eventually moved to Hillbrow, a residential area for white people, after receiving a tip from prostitutes regarding white people renting flats there. This is how she met Robert, a Swiss expat, who lived on her floor. In Robert, she saw the opposite of man she was used to: responsible and caring. She never wanted to marry, as it would be against her independent-woman creed, but she did want to have a baby. Despite the age difference (Robert was 46 and Patricia was 24), they got close enough to commit "the unspeakable crime of the apartheid age" in 1983.

Patricia understood the consequences of having a baby with a white man, so she chose to raise Trevor all by herself. She was fined and jailed by the South African authorities, but soon was released (marriages and sexual relations between races were strictly prohibited until 1985 when the Immorality Act was amended). Robert wasn't involved in raising little Trevor, but he wasn't kept aside by Patricia, so she let him see Trevor on a regular base. Soon after giving birth, Patricia moved back to Soweto, where they all lived for years. At this time, she was independent and perfectly capable of raising the boy herself, but she didn't want Trevor to grow alone. So, she brought him to a house full of her family. The house in Soweto was run by Patricia's mom, Frances, but also resided her older sister with her husband Dinky and their two children, Mlungisi and Bulelwa. Patricia's younger brother and her grandmother, who everyone called Koko, also resided there. By this time, Patricia was driving an old Volkswagen Beetle, which broke down a lot, but it still got her from Soweto to work and to church on Sundays.

For the first six years, she remained a single mother until she met a mechanic named Abel (Ngisaveni Abel Shingange), who fixed the old Volkswagen car. They got married in 1992 and had two more children, Andrew and Isaac. Although he was a great mechanic, Abel drank a lot and physically abused Patricia and Trevor a few times. When she complained to the police, they didn't want to interfere, considering that it was family problems that should be solved inside the family. Patricia divorced Abel in 1996, but they continued living together. In the meantime, the family operated a small garage called Mighty Mechanics, but the business had to close due to falling behind on payments. After losing the car shop, Abel became a more violent and abusive drunk, with Patricia and Trevor having to suffer. When Trevor became a comedian touring South Africa, Patricia was shot in the face by Abel; miraculously, she survived. He was arrested for attempted murder but released after just three years of prison. Abel still threatened Trevor, which encouraged him to leave South Africa for the US.

Trevor's Dad

Trevor's father was an enigma and hard to reveal by Trevor. That's why there are little-known things about him. He was the kind of person who was very discreet, rational, and calculated. He was the definition of Swiss— very clean and precise. Robert never got married, as he felt marriage was a form of control over the other partner and didn't want to be controlled. He was social and liked to travel, but he was also very private. He was never listed in a phonebook in South Africa. There aren't too many details related to Trevor's father. Robert was a Swiss expat, a skilled chef who worked in Montreal and New York and moved to South Africa in the late '70s. He opened a few bars and restaurants across South Africa while working for an international food-service company.

Robert was around 46 when he met Patricia, and at that time was operating a successful restaurant in Johannesburg, serving both white and black people with money. At one point, somebody filed a complaint, and the government tried to find ways to close down the restaurant. They tried with health-code violations and cleanliness, but they didn't succeed. According to Trevor, Robert is the kind of person who would check-in a hotel room and leave the room a lot cleaner than when he arrived. If the government couldn't catch him with such things, they came up with ridiculous restrictions, like having separated toilets for white, black, colored, and Indian people. He was given this choice, or to serve just white people. Robert refused and closed the restaurant. He never believed in racism and never respected the rules of the apartheid. Trevor believed that Africa was not the place to be for all the people hating black people, as it was their home, and you just can't come into somebody else's home and hate him.

Although he most likely had the money to invest in luxurious houses or cars, he was a frugal person who liked to keep it simple and not invest in fancy things. After apartheid ended, Robert moved from the Hillbrow area to Yeoville, a formerly quiet area of Johannesburg, which had become a vibrant neighborhood, with immigrants coming from Nigeria and Ghana. The immigrants also brought their food, culture, and music with them, so the main strip of Yeoville was packed with bars and restaurants. It was a place where Trevor didn't feel different, as the neighborhood was a mix of white, black, and colored people. Robert would see Trevor each Sunday when they spent time watching Formula 1 and cooking one of Trevor's favorite dishes, potato rösti. Most of these Sundays they spent in almost complete silence, as Robert was not the talking kind of guy. He mentioned something about his older sister, some other places he had been, steakhouses or restaurants, but that was about it. Trevor still preferred this kind of Sunday afternoon instead of going to all possible churches.

When Patricia got married to Abel, Trevor's visits were not frequent, as Abel didn't want to leave his wife and stepson on another man's doorstep. When Trevor was growing up, he was more interested in video games than spending time with his father. He never called Robert "dad," as he was instructed to do. The police would start to ask some questions, and this wouldn't be good for his mother and Robert. By the time Trevor was 13, many white people already left Yeoville, and many of Robert's German friends left this neighborhood for Cape Town. Also, Robert moved to Cape Town and lost contact with Patricia and Trevor for a while. As he was a discreet and mysterious person, Robert was difficult to track down when Patricia asked Trevor to find his father. Trevor contacted the Swiss Embassy, but they wouldn't reveal his location. Still, he received a postcard from his dad with the address in Cape Town. After more than ten years, Trevor and Robert met again. During the visit of his son, Robert never mentioned anything about himself; instead, they talked about Formula 1, sports, and politics.

Trevor was 24 when he last visited his father; by this time, he was already becoming a rising star in South Africa.

How They Met

Sexual relations and marriage between two different races were strictly forbidden during apartheid, these being a couple of the most severe crimes which could be done in this period. Babies born as a result of such relations couldn't be considered black or white; they were considered "colored," a different race group. Anyone with a drop of black blood would be considered automatically black in the U.S., but this was not the case in

South Africa. The first "colored" babies in South Africa came into this world nine months after the first Dutch boats sailed away. The authorities were trying to stop this phenomenon from spreading, as they wanted to keep the white race in South Africa pure. Therefore, a white man/woman couldn't form a family with a black woman/man, nor have children together. Any interracial kid as a result of a sexual relationship between a white person and a black person would be categorized as "colored" and couldn't live with both of his/her parents. The punishment for black people was a lot harsher than for the whites, but Patricia didn't consider all the consequences of having a mixed child during such a period.

After Patricia returned from Transkei, Xhosa homelands, she was already aware of what options in the labor market were available for black women. They could only work in factories or as maids—in other words, jobs with no skills. As she already experienced the factory work, she wasn't so thrilled of it, and she couldn't see herself listening to a white lady telling her what to do (and because she was a terrible cook), being a maid or a factory worker was out of the question. The political climate was favorable to her because of pressures from outside the Republic of South Africa; the government implemented some reforms which allowed black people to get low-level white collar jobs. Patricia already knew the English language well and attended a typing class, which helped her secure a position as a secretary at ICI, a multinational pharmaceutical company in Braamfontein, a suburb close to Johannesburg. When she started working over there, she was living in Soweto with her family, but she wasn't happy because she didn't have control over her earnings and had to support the whole household. At the age of 22, she ran away from home, determined to live in downtown Johannesburg. During that time, it was illegal for a black person to live in such an area; but she did find a way to do it.

The purpose of the authorities which implemented the apartheid was to build the Republic of South Africa for white people; that's why they had most of the properties in the country. However, this society couldn't function without the use of black people labor, so every white community needed to live close to a black community (called a township), from which people could come to work in the white area. It was the example of the housemaids who worked in the households of white people. If any black person didn't have a laborer status, he or she could be deported back to the homelands. Knowing this rule perfectly well, Patricia was determined to make it in downtown Johannesburg by sleeping and hiding in public restrooms and learning how to live downtown from prostitutes, who in many cases where Xhosa, just like her. They were the ones who taught her to wear a maid uniform when being downtown to avoid any questions from the police. These prostitutes also knew white men who were willing to rent a flat for prostitutes as a "place for work" in exchange for a cut from their activity. Patricia was not interested in such a deal, but already had a job which permitted her to earn enough money to pay rent in a flat. She found a nice place to stay in a neighborhood called Hillbrow. Her secret flat was number 203; on the same floor, just a few doors away, lived a tall, brown-eyed, Swiss-German named Robert.

Downtown Johannesburg was a very vibrant place to be, with plenty of expats from Germany or the Netherlands. There were many bars and restaurants, who served a more liberal clientele, both white and black, a clientele who didn't care about the rules or politics. It was a climate in which Patricia didn't know who to trust, as anyone could turn her to the police, thinking she was just a prostitute impersonating a maid. However, she found trustworthiness in the middle-aged Swiss man just down the hall. They spent time chatting at his flat (she would do the chatting as he was quieter and reserved), going to the nightclub to dance, and there was something between them, some chemistry. Patricia and Robert fell in love, and at that point, she wanted to have a baby. At first, he refused to take part in this, but eventually, he accepted, so nine months after Robert's acceptance, Patricia gave birth to Trevor on the 20th of February, 1984.

Delivering a "colored" baby at the Hillbrow Hospital raised some questions, like, who was the father? Patricia told them that the father was from Swaziland, so Trevor's birth certificate shows that he was born in KaNgwane (the semi-sovereign state of the Swazi people). Therefore, according to his birth certificate, Trevor is not Xhosa or Swiss. It shows that he was born in a different country.

Chapter 2:
Early Childhood Days

Grandmother's House

Apartheid was the perfect segregation tool the South African authorities used against the black population. Many black families were
separated most of the year, as the fathers were sent away to work in
mines or other factories, while the rest of the family stayed in the homeland.
Black children grew up without their fathers. In Trevor's case, apartheid
kept him away from his father for obvious reasons; therefore, he had grown
up in a world ruled by women. His early childhood memories were linked
to the township of Soweto, a huge black community right next to Johannesburg.

Women would be holding the community together, because the few
men over there were either unemployed, drunk, or up to no good. Religion
was a big part of their lives, trying to discipline their children in the
Christian religion. Soweto was a huge black ghetto, built to serve the white
population of Johannesburg. Black people were not allowed to live within
the city, but some of the women worked as maids inside the city. This place
was probably designed to be bombed, as there were only two roads in and
out. In Soweto lives more than one million black people, and such a place
had an economy, with minibus drivers taking black people to different
places in the city, auto mechanics, daycare, spaza shops (basic grocery stores
in garages), and shebeens (which were just unauthorized bars in someone's
back yard). Every family was allocated a small piece of land in this ghetto,
where they were allowed to build their property. However, the people were
too poor to build up a house, so they could only do it a bit at a time. They
could first build a brick wall, and then perhaps they could save money to

build another one and so on until the house was finished.

Trevor's grandmother (Frances) lived in Orlando East (a neighborhood of Soweto), and they would spend the time over there during holidays. His aunt (Sibongile) was also staying there during this time, with her two children Mlungisi and Bulelwa, so Trevor had children to play with. The neighborhood was filled with blackjacks (people working for the police, reporting anything suspicious), including Frances' neighbors. Therefore, Trevor was not allowed to play outside, where everyone could see him, as it wasn't safe for him. In a ghetto where everyone was black, a "colored" boy would immediately get the attention of other black people living there. When Trevor was just three years old, he managed to escape the yard by digging a hole beneath the gate of the driveway and ran away. The family immediately noticed that he was missing and organized a search party to track Trevor down. Of course, he didn't realize what he was doing, because he could have been taken away and his family deported. Frances' house and the yard was the play "universe" for Trevor, where he could play with his cousins.

It wasn't the time to have any friends, and he didn't know any other kids besides his cousins. When his mother was at work, he would play at home in his mother's tiny flat; and when being at this grandmother's house, he could play with his cousins. Trevor built up his imaginary world, as he was a voracious reader and played with the toys he had. He was a master of being alone and of entertaining himself.

A Deeply Religious Education

Religion was a big part of the Noah family, with Patricia being a Christian. Her mother, Frances, mixed the Christian faith with the old and traditional Xhosa beliefs. Many black people were easily converted to Christianity, especially Xhosa people, who thought that the religion of the oppressor might help their people to live a better life, just like the white people. Trevor was raised to be a deeply religious young boy, and his childhood involved a lot of going to church, sometimes at least four times per week. Monday didn't involve any religious activity; however, on Tuesday nights there was prayer meeting, Bible study was on Wednesday night, and there was Youth Church on Thursday. Friday and Saturday were off, but on Sunday, Trevor had to go to three different churches, as his mother wanted to show him different perspectives. Therefore, every Sunday was a tour of different churches, which would exhaust any young boy. Trevor could easily flag a church according to the people participating in the sermon. The first one was the mixed church, which offered jubilant praises to the Lord. Pastor McCauley was responsible for creating a very cheerful atmosphere and did his best onstage making the church cool. People were singing along, and if you didn't know the words, there was a Jumbotron nearby—it was Christian karaoke.

The next stop was the white church located in a fancy and very rich part of Johannesburg, which specialized in Bible analysis. Trevor learned the stories from the scripture, and, obviously, he enjoyed most the story of Noah and the flood (he felt he had a personal stake in this story because of his last name). Trevor enjoyed the Bible quizzes, which took place every week at the white church, as he was the best kid over there at these games.

The period spent at a black church was by far the longest because these sermons took too long, at least three or four hours. There was no air conditioning, no karaoke, just a long and boring service. Imagine around 500 old ladies in blue and white, just clutching their bibles and patiently waiting in the heat. However, in the fourth-hour, things became interesting as the pastor casts demons out of people. This spectacle was what Trevor enjoyed the most at the black church.

The Sunday tour of churches meant at least nine straight hours, which can be exhausting for a small boy, especially if it's really hard to stay in one place and he's more hyperactive. In his early childhood days, Patricia and Trevor were living in Eden Park, which was just a small neighborhood, a bit far from Johannesburg. The white church was a one-hour drive away, and then it took another 45 minutes to get to the mixed church, and another 45 minutes to get to the black church of Soweto. The journey back home was quite long, but sometimes they would stop at the white church again for a special evening service. The old Volkswagen Beetle was breaking down a lot and required fixing. However, if the car didn't start on a Sunday, this wouldn't stop Patricia from going to church—she would take mini-busses from one church to another.

One particular Sunday, when Trevor was nine years old, Patricia decided to go to church as she always did. She dressed up Andrew (her nine-month-old son) and headed for church. The old Volkswagen Beetle would not start, but she was still determined to go to church, despite her setbacks. They managed to make the whole tour using mini-busses: getting to the mixed church, then to the black church, and then to the white church. By the time the service ended at the white church, it was nine o'clock in the evening, it was dark outside, and the streets were empty. They were in the middle of a rich white neighborhood in Johannesburg, and there was no minibus in sight. At one point, they started to hitchhike, and it took forever until a car stopped and picked them up. Immediately after they were picked up, a minibus stopped just in front of the car, and the driver (of Zulu heritage) and another person started beating the driver of the car. Patricia made them stop and promised to get on the minibus if they leave the man alone, as he was helping her. Very often the minibus drivers were gangsters who had established routes, and no one had the right to steal their routes. Anyone caught doing this was most likely killed, so the reaction was somehow not out of the ordinary.

In the minibus, Patricia was lectured about being in the same car with strange men, especially when she had a "colored" boy. She couldn't stand any lecture from strange men, and she told him to mind his own business. When the driver heard her talking in Xhosa, he was outraged. In the Zulu men's perception, the Xhosa women were unfaithful and promiscuous. He started insulting Patricia, and everything escalated to the point that he called Patricia a slut and said he would teach her a lesson tonight. At this point, Patricia was very clear that the driver intended to kill her, as he was speeding and never stopping, only slowing down in the intersection to check for traffic. At one traffic light, she opened the sliding door and threw Trevor as far as she could, took Andrew, and jumped out of the minibus. They started running until they made it to a gas station where they called the police.

First Naughty Behaviors

The time Trevor spent in Soweto at his grandma's house was the time when he would do some naughty stuff. He couldn't afford to be naughty when he was with his mom; but when she was not around, it was the perfect time to misbehave. Since his family treated him like a white child, he enjoyed the benefits of being "white" in a black family. He received special treatment, and no matter what he did, he escaped unpunished. When he was five, Trevor was playing doctor with his cousins, Mlungisi and Bulelwa, him being the doctor and them his patients. He was using a set of matches to operate on Bulelwa's ear, and he accidentally perforated his cousin's eardrum. Bulelwa started to cry and bleed. Frances rushed in the yard to see what was happening and immediately patched up Bulelwa's ears, making sure it was no longer bleeding. Then the angry grandmother just took out a belt and beat both Bulelwa and Mlungisi. She didn't touch Trevor, who caused this incident. She was scared to beat a white kid because they could turn to different colors. When you beat any black kid, they stay black, but if you beat Trevor, he could turn red, blue, yellow, or green. Trevor wasn't afraid of getting beaten by anyone in his family; the only person he truly feared was his mother, as she didn't want to spoil Trevor and believed in a very disciplinary education (sometimes a bit violent).

Soweto was a place just for the black community, having a different heritage and coming from the homelands. Trevor was the only "colored" person over there, but he was considered white by everyone. He was considered an anomaly and couldn't have any friends at all. The black ghetto of Soweto was like a melting pot, with black people of different tribes living together, and different languages were spoken. Patricia and her family had a Xhosa heritage, so they spoke this language. Other people were speaking Zulu, Tsonga, or Sotho. Back then, the English language could make the difference from having a job and being unemployed, but Patricia spoke English well. She also learned German because of Robert, as well as Afrikaans, the language of the oppressor. Trevor became a true polyglot, learning as many languages as possible, which was a useful thing, as he could blend in with different ethnic groups. The color of his skin wouldn't change, but he could be the social chameleon who could speak in plenty of languages spoken in South Africa. Trevor learned to speak English, Xhosa, Zulu, Tswana, Sotho, Tsonga, Afrikaans, and German. Patricia raised Trevor with English as the main language, because she wanted him to master this language, as it was the language of opportunity in South Africa.

Chapter 3: Education

Maryvale College vs. H.A Jack Primary School

The first school Trevor attended was Maryvale College, an expensive private Catholic school. The multinational company Patricia was working for offered scholarships for underprivileged families, and she managed to get one for Trevor. The classes were taught by nuns, and there were kids of different races and social backgrounds. It was the first time he was seeing people of different races together, something which he didn't think possible until that point. Maryvale College kept the truth from any student attending this school, as in real life, people of all races would not stay together as they did at this Catholic school. However, things would change when Trevor had to leave the Catholic school at the end of the sixth grade and go to H.A. Jack Primary, a government school. He took an aptitude test and was placed in honor classes. In his class, he only noticed one or two black kids, an Indian kid, and almost thirty white kids. He thought he attended a mostly white school until he went into recess and saw the reality for the first time. The playground looked like a battlefield, with clearly separated sides, (the only difference was that the kids were not fighting against each other). There were the white kids in a corner (most of his colleagues were there); and on the other side, several groups of black people. There he was, standing in the middle of the playground, not knowing which side to pick.

His Indian colleague came to him and started having a conversation. He discovered that Trevor could speak several South African languages, so he encouraged Trevor to go to each black group and talk to them. Trevor was welcomed by the black kids and was able to communicate with them in Zulu or Xhosa. The recess period made him understand where he truly belonged. He immediately realized that his place was not amongst the white people of the A classes, so he went to see the school counselor and demanded to be put in the B classes where the black kids were. Although he was told that if he quit the A classes he's basically renouncing the opportunities which he would have by belonging in these classes, Trevor decided that he would rather take his chances with the people he liked (and risk being held back), instead of being with the people he didn't know.

H.A. Jack Primary convinced Trevor to choose a side, and he chose black. Even though his father was white and in the white Sunday school he got along well with white kids; he didn't belong with the other white kids of his primary school. He was raised as black, his cousins, mom, and grandmother were black, and he felt welcomed with the black kids. They didn't consider him black, and Trevor wasn't part of their tribe, but he knew their language, and that was good enough for them. He was 11 years old when he had to decide regarding the side to choose, as he was seeing the country the first time exactly as it was, although by this time apartheid had ended. Still, old habits die very hard, and the segregation continued involuntarily. Kids were not used to sticking together, so exactly like the apartheid days, they had separate groups.

This was the period when Trevor could socialize and make some true friends for the first time in his life, as he no longer had to hide because of who he was. He could now blend in with all the black groups, just like a chameleon.

A Little "Devil"

Trevor was a voracious eater, too, not just a reader. He was always eating faster than his cousins and would eat almost anything. Everybody in the family expected him to become obese, but this didn't happen. They all thought Trevor had worms. However, he was hyperactive and consumed most of his excess energy. Running for him was like a play, so he would run most of the time, and that's why he got the reputation of a very fast runner. Patricia would take him to parks and run him out until he was out of energy.

He was thrown a Frisbee, and he would run to catch it and bring it back, just like white people would do with their dogs. Trevor recalled that, "my mom was training me like a dog." [1]

He would put all that energy up to no good. At Catholic school, he would take the magnifying glasses out of the projectors, or fill the piano with foam from the fire extinguishers. When somebody wanted to play the piano, that foam from the piano would explode out if it. Trevor was constant trouble and was fascinated with knives and fire. It was the time of movies like Rambo and Crocodile Dundee when every kid would dream of having knives just like he had seen in all these movies. Fire was Trevor's favorite, especially fireworks. Anyone would agree that they are child play, but Trevor didn't care. South Africa was celebrating Guy Fawkes Day in November (Bonfire Day in the UK) when everyone bought fireworks for celebration. Patricia would buy a mini-arsenal of such fireworks. Trevor just loved this day, and he wanted to build a huge firework by himself by getting all the gunpowder out of the fireworks. He filled an empty plant pot with gunpowder when he noticed a Black Cat firecracker. These firecrackers normally are lit, and they explode after that, but Trevor wanted to break them in half and use them as a mini flamethrower. The match dropped in the pot of gunpowder, and the whole thing exploded into Trevor's face. He lied to his mother about playing with fire, but the evidence was there; the explosion burnt off Trevor's eyebrows and about an inch of his front hair.

From an adult perspective, he was trouble, destructive, a South African "Dennis the Menace," but Trevor had a different view. Destruction was not his purpose: he considered that he created fire, instead of burning his facial hair; he wasn't breaking the projectors from his school, he was creating chaos to check the reaction of people. Trevor was that kind of kid that if you told him not to do something, he would agree with you and minutes later, he would do that exact "something" he was asked not to do. He didn't escape unpunished, as his mom would beat him for most of his misbehaviors.

Social Segregation at School

After being transferred from Maryvale College to H.A. Jack Primary, Trevor started to find out how real life felt amongst kids of all kinds of races. If the Catholic School was like an "oasis" where everyone was getting along well to respect the authoritarian rules of the school, at the primary school he experienced the real life from the end of apartheid period. He was able to see segregation, hatred, and mistrust between groups. He had to pick a side, as he couldn't remain neutral for a longer period. Since he was raised as black and was used to black people, he chose the black side, being the "colored" kid who would try to embrace the black values to blend in with the other black kids. Just like growing up in Eden Park, the mixed neighborhood, he found out that if he had respect for the various black cultures, the kids from different black tribes would respect him and would consider him part of their group. He was the insider from outside the group, being able to integrate into the group and speak the language, but having a lighter skin color.

During the Catholic school days, Trevor was probably the naughtiest kid in there, but his deeds were also like a cry to be noticed by the others, to be seen as a cool kid while revolting against the authority. The tight grip of strict rules wasn't something normal at H.A. Jack Primary because these were the final days of apartheid, and Trevor was able to see reality uncensored. He was always friendly and open to new friendships but didn't have the chance of making new friends. Trevor spent only three years in this primary school, from the sixth grade to the eighth grade. He attended the courses of Sandringham School, which was a Model C school, a mixture between public and private, getting kids of all races and from all kind of social ranks. There were black, white, mixed kids, and even Chinese and Indian kids. It was like a mini-universe or a salad-bowl. There were rich, middle-class, and working-class white children.

Then there were rich black kids (newly rich as these were the early days of the post-apartheid era), middle-class black kids, and black kids from the ghettos. Also, you could see some colored kids, a few Indian children, and some Chinese kids. Sandringham School was a huge place, with playgrounds, sports fields, tennis courts, and a swimming pool, having more than 1000 kids. Even though apartheid was over, it didn't mean that segregation was over. Kids would still stay grouped according to races, but this time you could notice that they were also grouped according to the social background. According to the activity they practiced, the children would group differently. Black kids were usually playing soccer, so they were sticking together, while white kids were usually playing tennis, mixed kids were playing cricket, and so on. Just like in the American high-school movies, you would notice the matrics hanging out together (they were the equivalent of seniors in South Africa), beautiful, popular girls were having their very own group, and the computer geeks. Nobody was imposing this, but this was voluntary segregation. Trevor felt again that he was caught in the middle, as he had to pick a group to blend in with. There were some colored kids, but as he already experienced in Eden Park, these kids hated him because was trying to become black (and they didn't), and he didn't speak their language (Afrikaans) well. He didn't have any conflicts with white kids and got along quite well with them (from Sunday church and Catholic School); but still, he didn't believe he belonged with them. He knew them and was close enough to them not to get bullied by them, but hanging out with them required money, which Trevor didn't have at the time. He could mostly relate with the poor black kids, who were originally from the ghettos.

However, these kids were living in ghettos like Soweto, Alexandra, or Tembisa, which were not in Trevor's way when he had to go home or to go back to school. They had their very specific group, as they would go home together, come back to school together, and spend their free time together. His family didn't have too much at that point, so gas was a luxury, and Trevor couldn't visit the kids in the ghettos. He had to take a long walk each day, from home to school and back, which made him late for classes almost every day. When this would happen, he had to sign in the detention file, so he spent after school in detention. Most of the day, Trevor would spend it at school or on his way to school and back home. He was normally on the detention list, and every day at the beginning of the break, the prefect would call out the persons for detention, and Trevor already had a reputation of getting in detention all the time, so this was a way the other kids would remember him. It was like the Oscars or the Emmy Awards, Trevor being the one with the most "awards."

The schools in South Africa didn't have a cafeteria, so there wasn't a warm lunch guaranteed for each student. Sandringham School had something called a tuck shop, which was a small canteen that didn't have enough food for all the students from this school. This caused a "race for survival," because if you weren't the first over there to buy the good stuff, you had to stay in line for a long period, and by the time you got to the counter, you wouldn't have any good food left to choose from. Trevor saw in this the perfect opportunity to make some friends and interact with different types of students. This was a task for the undisputed running champion of Maryvale College, as nobody could run faster than him. He could outrun every single kid in school and be the first one at the tuck shop. Everyone else noticed his skills, so other kids would come to him and ask Trevor to buy something for them from the shop, as they couldn't get there in time to buy what they wanted. This is how he became the tuck-shop guy; the person many kids would look up to buy their favorite snacks from that shop. Trevor had his very own clientele and started making some money out of his food run. His clients were willing to pay for this service, as they wanted to enjoy the recess and not spend it in line at the tuck shop. Trevor's favorite clients were the rich, pudgier kids, who simply couldn't run fast to position themselves properly in the line to get their favorite snacks. Everybody was asking for hot dogs, muffins, and Cokes, and he would make a bit of cash doing the food run every day. When recess was approaching, Trevor asked: "Place your orders!"

This activity made him famous in the school, and now he felt confident approaching any group. He was able to play sports with the jocks, discuss computers and the latest video games with the school nerds, or dance with the ghetto black kids. He could easily chat, laugh, tell jokes, and make deliveries to all groups in the playground. At a modern-day party, the guy with the weed or with the booze would always be welcome; he was not part of the group, but he could temporarily join the group in exchange of what he had to offer. Trevor was much like the weed dealer type, but instead of weed, he had something else to offer to all the groups: his food delivering services and of course, his humor. He learned from his teenage years that humor was the key to making new friends. Trevor wouldn't overstay his welcome; he would pop in, tell a few jokes, lift the spirits of those in the group, and then he would go ahead to a different group to do the same thing. He didn't belong to a particular group—not popular, but not an outcast.

Teddy

Not all the kids he could relate to were staying far away from school in the black ghetto. At Sandringham High School, Trevor met a charming and funny kid, and soon they became close friends. His name was Teddy, and he was living in Linksfield, a white neighborhood very close to the school. His mother was a maid, serving for a white family in that suburb, so he was living with her in that wealthy part of the city. Trevor and Teddy were much alike: they were both the family terrors, and they were extremely naughty. They became "partners in crime," serving a lot of detention time because of all the trouble they caused.

Teddy lived 45 minutes away from Trevor, which was quite a lot to walk; but for Trevor, their time spent together was worth it. They just loved to hang around at the Balfour Park Shopping Mall; but they weren't doing any shopping over there, they were just up to no good. The mall had plenty of shops, but also a food court and a cinema. Hanging out around the cinema when all the other shops were closed was something they loved. The cinema was still open, as they were showing the last movie of the day, and the stationery shop was also closed. With no one around, they found out that they could get some chocolate out of the chocolate rack if they reached with the hand through the trellis. They had some delicious alcohol-filled chocolates with rum, brandy, or whiskey (they were just crazy about them), which they decided to repeat every weekend.

On one Saturday, when Trevor was sneaking in his hand in the chocolate rack, a mall cop came from around the corner and saw somebody stealing chocolates. The main disadvantage of shoplifting so close to your home is that you are a very familiar figure for them, definitely not a stranger. The guards already knew them, since they spent too much time inside the mall. Worse than that, they also knew Patricia, as she was doing the banking over there. This meant extra trouble for Trevor because if his mom found out what he was doing, the consequences for him would be terrible. So their only hope, in this case, was not to be seen (their face) and not to get caught. Immediately the chase was on, and even though Trevor and Teddy could run, other mall guards would join the chase. They were not like the American stereotype of mall cops, fat and too lazy to run. They were very fast, so Trevor and Teddy couldn't lose them. The chase moved to the parking lot, as the boys were ducking behind cars not to be seen or caught, and then it moved to the nearby streets. Trevor was terrified, but also enjoyed the moment, as he always took running like some game he was winning every time. He didn't want to lose today, not in his neighborhood. Trevor knew these streets like his own home, and after passing the fire station, they made a left turn which led them into a dead end and then a metal fence. He knew that the fence was cut and he thought he could squeeze through that hole in the fence, escape on the empty field behind the mall and then hide at his home. A grown-up wouldn't fit in that hole, and unfortunately, Teddy didn't want to squeeze through that hole. They split, half of the mall cops chasing Teddy, the other half chasing Trevor. Just like planned, Trevor made it through the hole and arrived safely home, but Teddy was eventually caught. They didn't meet on Monday at school, but Teddy's parents showed up after school to Trevor's home, telling Patricia that their son got arrested for shoplifting, but there was another kid with him, and according to Teddy, that kid was not Trevor. Patricia was convinced that Trevor was involved, but Teddy's parents assured her that Trevor wasn't involved.

The next day at school, Trevor was summoned to the Principal's office, and he knew straight away this wasn't good news. He had the video footage of the chase, and since Trevor was Teddy's best friend, the Principal was hoping that Trevor would help him identify the other boy. The footage from the security camera was far from being clear, and it was also black and white. If they could easily distinguish Teddy, who had dark skin, nobody could recognize Trevor on this footage, as he was shown as white. They were convinced that the other boy who was running with Teddy was a white kid and they were hoping Trevor could identify him. Trevor couldn't recognize any white boy in the footage and didn't admit that he was the one in the video. He was eventually sent back to class and was extremely worried that he would be recognized at one point. Due to the flaws of technology from that period, Trevor was not arrested for shoplifting. His lighter skin showed up as white on the black and white footage, so nobody who watched the video was able to recognize him.

Chapter 4:
A Special Relationship

Written Correspondence

Trevor and Patricia always had a special relationship. She always tried to control him, but Trevor was not the submissive type. If Trevor had youth and excessive energy on his side, Patricia could keep him in line by being cunning and develop all sorts of strategies. A good example would be when they went shopping, and Trevor would want a special thing, like a toffee apple. She would remain immune to his nagging and wouldn't want to buy that toffee apple until she told him to grab one. Trevor went to pick the toffee apple, put it on the counter and the salesman looked very suspicious at him, telling Trevor to wait his turn, as he was serving a customer (Patricia). As Trevor would describe it in his book:

"Add this toffee apple, please," I said.

The cashier looked at me skeptically. "Wait your turn, boy. I'm still helping this lady."

"No," I said, "she's buying it for me."

My mother turned to me, "Who's buying it for you?"

"You're buying it for me."

"No, no. Why doesn't your mother buy it for you?"

"What? My mother? You are my mother."

"I'm your mother? No, I'm not your mother. Where's your mother?"

I was so confused. *"You're* my mother."

The cashier looked at her, looked back at me, looked at her again. She shrugged, like, *I have no idea what that kid's talking about.* Then she looked at me like she'd never seen me before in her life.

"Are you lost, little boy? Where's your mother?"

"Yeah," the cashier said, "where's your mother?"

I pointed at my mother. "She's my mother."

"What? She can't be your mother, boy. She's black. Can't you see?"

My mom shook her head. "Poor little colored boy lost his mother. What a shame."

I panicked. Was I crazy? Is she not my mother? I started bawling. " *You're* my mother. *You're* my mother. *She's* my mother. *She's* my mother."

She shrugged again. "So sad. I hope he finds his mother."

The cashier nodded. She paid him, took our groceries, and walked out of the shop. I dropped the toffee apple, ran out behind her in tears, and caught up to her at the car. She turned around, laughing hysterically as she'd got me good.

"Why are you crying?" she asked.

"Because you said you weren't my mother. Why did you say you weren't my mother?"

"Because you wouldn't shut up about the toffee apple. Now get in the car. Let's go." [2]

As Trevor grew up, Patricia would use different tactics to keep him in line, since having a serious discussion with him could take forever. If she had to tell him to do something, Trevor was quick to argue, so to stop endless debates, Patricia would leave notes if there were chores to do. She would write them on a letter and slip them under the door, just like a landlord with his tenant.

"Dear Trevor,

"Children, obey your parents in everything, for this pleases the Lord."

—Colossians 3:20

There are certain things I expect from you as my child and as a young man. You need to clean your room. You need to keep the house clean. You need to look after your school uniform. Please, my child, I ask you. Respect my rules so that I may also respect you. I ask you now, please go and do the dishes and do the weeds in the garden.

Yours sincerely,

Mom" [3]

Trevor was good with debating, but he also had a talent when it came to expressing himself by writing letters, a talent which he inherited from his mother. He would use his business correspondence skills and write back to her:

"To Whom It May Concern:

Dear Mom,

I have received your correspondence earlier. I am delighted to say that I am ahead of schedule on the dishes, and I will continue to wash them in an hour or so. Please note that the garden is wet, and so I cannot do the weeds at this time, but please be assured this task will be completed by the end of the weekend. Also, I completely agree with what you are saying with regard to my respect levels, and I will maintain my room to a satisfactory standard.

Yours sincerely,

Trevor" [4]

These are just some examples of polite letters, but when Trevor was being naughty or got in trouble at school, the letters would mention punishment.

"Dear Trevor,

"Foolishness is bound up in the heart of a child; the rod of discipline will remove it far from him."

—Proverbs 22:15

Your school marks this term have been very disappointing, and your behavior in class continues to be disruptive and disrespectful. It is clear from your actions that you do not respect me. You do not respect your teachers. Learn to respect the women in your life. The way you treat me and the way you treat your teachers will be the way you treat other women in the world. Learn to buck that trend now, and you will be a better man because of it. Because of your behavior, I am grounding you for one week. There will be no television and no video games.

Yours sincerely,

Mom" [5]

Naturally, Trevor would consider these punishments unfair, and he would like to discuss them with his mom, but she wouldn't agree. Patricia knew that this would lead to an endless debate, so she forced Trevor to write down in a letter what he had to say regarding these punishments.

"To Whom It May Concern:

Dear Mom,

First of all, this has been a particularly tough time in school, and for you to say that my marks are bad is extremely unfair, especially considering the fact that you yourself were not very good in school, and I am, after all, a product of yours, and so in part you are to blame because if you were not good in school, why would I be good in school because genetically we are the same. Gran always talks about how naughty you were, so obviously my naughtiness comes from you, so I don't think it is right or just for you to say any of this.

Yours sincerely,

Trevor" [6]

Patricia wouldn't agree with her son's arguments because she firmly believed that her behavior during her childhood days was not an excuse for

Trevor to behave like that. She would tear the letter, and all this would be back in forth for more days, as she had to reply to Trevor's letter, he had to reply, and so on.

His "Naughtiness"

Like any black parent, Patricia believed in the concept of tough love, as she would discipline young Trevor using harsh methods. Punishments were applied for minor offenses; when it was something serious, the full-scale beating was applied. Trevor would have to run from his angry mom and, although he was very fast, his mom could still catch him (until he grew up). They were like the springbok (the second fastest mammal) and the cheetah. However, when she did catch him, all hell broke loose for Trevor because unlike his grandmother, his mom wouldn't hesitate to beat him up. This was love through discipline, and Trevor couldn't expect less for a kid who was destroying pianos or projectors at school. The steam would run off quickly, and Patricia's anger disappeared quickly, as she was calling him to get dinner and then watching Rescue 911 together.

Trevor was not the most disciplined child at Maryvale College, and the nuns had some interest for him. Whenever he did something naughty, the nuns would rap his knuckles with the edge of a metal ruler. When he was cursing, they would wash his mouth with soap. Serious offenses would get him in the principal's office, where he would receive repeated beats over his behind with a flat rubber, which looked like the sole of a shoe. These beatings were mild, as the principal was afraid not to hit the troubled young boy too hard. On one occasion, Trevor was thinking "Man, if only my mom was like this" [7] and he started laughing. The principal thought that there was something wrong with Trevor, as he was enjoying the beatings. That's why he sent Trevor to a psychologist to be examined. The shrink examined him, but he was under the impression that Trevor could become an excellent criminal or someone good at catching criminals, as he could always see some loopholes in the law or flaws with any rule and find a way around them. There wasn't anything wrong with Trevor (according to the psychologist), he was just good at being creative, independent, and had a lot of energy to put his plans into action.

Trevor never understood the purpose of communion for him, at Friday mass, as he had to kneel, stand, sit, kneel, stand, and sit again; but at the end, he would remain hungry, as he wasn't allowed to take communion (Trevor was not Catholic). He would starve watching the other kids eating the "body of Christ" and drinking "Jesus' blood," and always argued with nuns and priests why he was not receiving the communion. He just loved grape juice and crackers. His argument with them would be like:

"Only Catholics can eat Jesus's body and drink Jesus's blood, right?"

"Yes."

"But Jesus wasn't Catholic."

"No."

"Jesus was Jewish."

"Well, yes."

"So you're telling me that if Jesus walked into your church right now, Jesus would not be allowed to have the body and blood of Jesus?"

"Well...uh...um..." [8]

He never received a reply he was satisfied with. As he thought that he deserved to receive communion, one day Trevor decided to take matters into his own hands and get the "blood and body of Christ." He went behind the altar, drank an entire bottle of grape juice, and had an entire bag of Eucharist to compensate for all the times he didn't receive any communion. Trevor always fought that the communion rule didn't make any sense, so from his perspective he wasn't breaking any rules. When he was getting all the "blood and body of Christ" Trevor wasn't alone, as other kids saw him. In confession, one of the kids told the priest what Trevor had done, and the priest handed over Trevor to the principal. *"You've* broken the rules. That's confidential information. The priest isn't supposed to repeat what you say in confession," [9] Trevor said.

The principal was shocked:

"What kind of a sick person would eat all of Jesus's body and drink all of Jesus's blood?"

"A hungry person," [10] Trevor replied.

This incident brought Trevor the second visit to the shrink; the third time was in the sixth grade when a kid was bullying him and was threatening to beat him up. Trevor brought his knives to school, not to use them, but to have and intimidate the other kid. This was the first time the principal mentioned something about expelling Trevor, giving him an ultimatum to straighten up. This was a clear signal to get out of there, so he told the principal he didn't want to be there anymore. This is how Catholic school ended for Trevor.

This time he didn't get in trouble at home, as his mom left the job she had at ICI (the multinational pharmaceutical company), so Trevor lost the scholarship for the Catholic school. Paying for an expensive, private Catholic school had become a burden for Patricia. She would back up Trevor and support him, convinced that the school was overreacting. She discussed with the principal, to find out the official position of the school related to the incidents her son was involved in. "Let me get this straight," she told the principal. "You're punishing a child because he *wants* Jesus's body and Jesus's blood? Why shouldn't he have those things? Of course, he should have them." [11]

She also considered ridiculous the fact that Trevor was sent to see a psychologist for laughing when the principal beat him.

"Ms. Noah, your son was laughing while we were hitting him."

"Well, clearly you don't know how to hit a kid. That's your problem, not mine. Trevor's never laughed when I've hit him; I can tell you." [12]

The Catholic Church was much like the apartheid itself, having strict rules and being very authoritarian, an authority which relied on many rules that didn't make any sense. Questioning these rules was Trevor's specialty, and his mother would back him up because she grew up with these kinds of rules, and she would also not see any logic to them. The only authority she recognized was God, and God spoke to us through the Bible. "God is love, and the Bible is truth—everything else was up for debate." [13] Trevor learned from her to "challenge the authority and to question the system." [14]

Fire Obsession

Trevor's picture as a child should have been in a dictionary next to the word "naughty," as his misbehavior exceeded everything that you could imagine. When there wasn't any adult supervision, he was always up to no good. Besides his family or the people from school, there was another person who was about to discover just how naughty Trevor was. When he was seven, his mother had already started dating Abel, who was living in the suburbs, renting the garage from a white family household. This was one way that black people could live close by white families if they rented the server's quarters or, in this case, the garage. He turned the garage into a cottage-type home, with a bed and a hot plate. The garage was in the Orange Grove suburb, close to the Catholic school, but also close to Patricia's workplace. The old Volkswagen Beetle car was the reason Patricia was dating Abel, as he was a skilled mechanic that she would visit every time she had issues with the car. Abel later became Trevor's stepdad. So the second-hand car was responsible for Patricia's marriage. She spent a lot of time with this mechanic, and even Trevor liked him at first. Abel sometimes slept at their home, and then they would sleep at his garage in Orange Grove. They were all getting very close and started to become a family.

The white house, which had the garage, also had a server's quarter in the backyard, where the black maid lived and where Trevor played with her son. Naturally, his fascination for fire meant trouble. On one afternoon, when everyone was at work, Trevor was playing with the maid's son, and he was teaching him how to burn his name on wooden plates. This was something he practiced plenty of times, so he felt comfortable to teach this boy the secret behind the procedure. He loved using the magnifying glass to focus the sunlight on the wooden plates until they started to burn and then slowly moving it to burn the plates in the shape of letters. They were in the server's shack, which was more of a wooden shed, with buckets of old paint, wooden stairs, turpentine, and a mattress filled with straws. The sun was beaming strongly through the window, so Trevor could easily engrave his name on a wooden plate indoors, but he also had matches if he needed any help to burn his name on those plates. At one point, they went outside the shed to get a snack, and they left the magnifying glass and the matches on the straw mattress. The shed had something like a self-closing system from the inside so that they couldn't get back in. They decided to play in the yard until they noticed smoke coming out from the shed. It caught fire as the magnifying glass lit the matches, so the straw mattress was on fire, and soon the old buckets of paint and the wooden stairs rapidly started to burn. The flames moved quickly, the roof was already on fire, and then the main house was on fire and also the garage. A neighbor alerted the fire brigade, but they couldn't save anything from the fire, as all the property was already burnt.

The white family remained speechless when they saw what remained of their house. When they asked the maid what happened, she said that Trevor had matches. They didn't do anything to him, didn't call the police, and didn't sue Patricia. However, the white family did ask Abel to pack his things and move out. From that moment, Abel lived with Patricia and Trevor in Eden Park. When they arrived back home, Patricia and Abel argued intensively. "Your son has burned down my life!" Abel said. Trevor's mom was simply shocked, as being naughty was one thing, but burning down a house was something that she could never have imagined Trevor being capable of. Trevor still considered himself to be innocent. "There were matches, and there was a magnifying glass, and there was a mattress and then, clearly, a series of unfortunate events. Things catch fire sometimes. That's why there's a fire brigade." [15] This incident gave Trevor a feared reputation among his family; one of his uncles calling him "Terror" instead of his name.

His cousin, Mlungisi, was the opposite of Trevor, being a good kid. He still doesn't understand how Trevor survived all these years, being such a naughty boy. Trevor received severe beatings from his mother for all the times he got in serious trouble. If his cousin would behave exemplarily after being punished and would always follow the rules never to experience the punishment again, Trevor was different. He inherited from Patricia the ability to move on and forget the pain in his life. "I remember the thing that caused the trauma, but I don't hold on to the trauma. I never let the memory of something painful prevent me from trying something new." [16]

He would never overthink the beatings he received from his mother or from life itself because doing this would stop him from forcing the limits and breaking the rules.

Chapter 5:
How to Look Alike and
to Be Different

The "Colored" Type

A partheid was the system which segregated and categorized people, using a divide-and-conquer model. There was a lot of hatred and mistrust amongst the races and tribes of South Africa, so they were never united against the common oppressor. The "colored" persons were considered almost-whites, having rights and privileges that black people didn't have. If the whites were first-class citizens, the "colored" were second-class citizens, being called by the Afrikaners *amperbaas* ("the almost-boss"). Trevor has an interesting opinion regarding this situation: "You're *almost* there. You're *so close.* You're *this close* to being white. Pity your grandfather couldn't keep his hands off the chocolate, eh? But it's not your fault you're colored, so keep trying; because if you work hard enough, you can erase this taint from your bloodline. Keep on marrying lighter and whiter, and don't touch the chocolate and maybe, *maybe,* someday, if you're lucky, you can become white." [17]

It may sound strange and ridiculous, but this happened. Under apartheid, mixed people could apply for a white person status. If the skin was light enough, the hair was straight enough, and the accent was polished enough, a "colored" person could be upgraded to white. However, nothing comes without a price. The white status meant that the mixed person had to denounce its people, history and to leave your darker-skin relatives and friends behind.

The official definition of a white person under apartheid would sound like this: "one who in appearance is a white person who is generally not accepted as a colored person; or is generally accepted as a white person and is not in appearance obviously a white person." [18] The pencil test was one of the tests a colored person had to pass (in front of the examiners) to be categorized as white. If they put a pen into your hair, the pen had to fall in order for you to be classified as white. If it stayed in, you were black. The examiners were also looking for things like how high were the cheekbones, or when examining the nose, how broad it was. They were influential because in their pen determined the future of millions. They could decide where you can live, what jobs or privileges you could have, or whom you could marry. Such a regime could split up families. For instance, if a family of white people had a darker than usual child, even though both of the parents provided documents that they were white, the baby was categorized as colored, and the parents would have to make a decision; whether they renounce their white status and go live as a family in the colored area, or they could split, with the mother taking the child to live in the ghetto and the father working in the white area to support them.

A strange perception during these horrible times was that the black people were holding down the colored ones, it's like their blood was tainted by the black people. They didn't want the blacks aspiring to be white, to use the coloredness as an excuse to benefit from all the perks of whiteness.

"That's what apartheid did: it convinced every group that it was because of the other race that they didn't get into the club. It's basically the bouncer at the door telling you, "We can't let you in because of your friend Darren and his ugly shoes." So you look at Darren and say, "screw you, Black Darren. You're holding me back." Then, when Darren goes up, the bouncer says, "no, it's actually your friend Sizwe and his weird hair." So Darren says, "screw you, Sizwe," and now everyone hates everyone. But the truth is that none of you were ever getting into that club."—as Trevor points out. [19]

The Mulberry Tree Incident

Eden Park was a small suburb quite far from Johannesburg, which was full of colored people. Although everyone looked like Trevor, they were very different, so he felt that he could never blend in over there. First of all, most of them were speaking Afrikaans, while Trevor could barely speak this language at this point. He was raised in a black family and black neighborhood, so he spoke better African languages like Xhosa (the native language of his mother) and Zulu (which was very similar to Xhosa), both of them making clicking sounds. Most importantly, he spoke English as his main language, so the other kids in this neighborhood thought he was showing off and trying to be superior. A good lesson he learned in his period spent in South Africa was that it was always "easier to be an insider as an outsider than to be an outsider as an insider." [20] This is all about embracing the culture and language of the people you're referring to. For example, if a black person adapts in the white community, plays golf, and does other white-related activities, white people would appreciate him. Also, a white person embracing the black culture while living in a black community is also something appreciated. However, a black person acting white in a black community, or a white person acting black in a white community would make that person experience ridicule and hatred by the rest of the community.

In this particular case, people could accept the outsider trying to blend into their world, but they could never forgive a fellow tribe member who would be disavowing the tribe. Trevor met two kinds of colored people in Eden Park (as he didn't have to hide in the yard anymore): the ones who hated him for his black influence and the ones who hated him for his white influence. Most of the colored people were supposed to speak Afrikaans, which was a language that Trevor didn't master yet. When the first type of colored people heard him speaking in Xhosa or Zulu, they would insult him by calling him a bushman, as a reference to his primitiveness. The others hated Trevor for his knowledge of the English language, as he was supposed to speak Afrikaans. Speaking fluent English, others were probably thought that he was trying to show off, trying to show he's superior. The reality was cruel, and he wasn't able to make any friend, as everyone else would hate him.

Trevor recalls an incident when he had a brand new bike during the summer holidays. His cousin, Mlungisi, used to visit him during these holidays and they took turns riding the bike just around the block. One time when Trevor rode the bike, a cute colored girl stopped him and asked him if she could ride the bike. He was a bit shocked, and he thought she wanted to become his friend. He let her ride the bike for a few feet, then another kid came out of nowhere, stopped her, climbed on the bike, and took off. Trevor was simply mesmerized by the fact that a cute girl spoke to him, that he completely ignored that somebody just has stolen the bike. When Mlungisi asked where the bike was, Trevor replied:

"Trevor, you've been robbed," he said. "Why didn't you chase them?"

"I thought they were being nice. I thought I'd made a friend." [21]

Mlungisi may have been a super good kid, but he was also Trevor's protector. He went to find the kids, and after 30 minutes returned with the bike.

Being a lonely kid and not having any friends made Trevor a vulnerable kid for bullies, and that's why he was bullied quite often. One afternoon when he was playing by himself, running in the neighborhood (just like he always did), he noticed a group of five or six eating berries from a mulberry tree. They were all around 12 or 13 (older than him). Trevor went over there to pick some berries to take home, when one of them took the berries out of his hands and smashed them into the ground, causing the other kids to laugh. He was already so used to bullying, that he ignored the whole thing and continued picking berries. Their ring leader didn't expect this reaction from Trevor, so he insulted him by calling him a "bushman," but Trevor still ignored him. The other kids started throwing berries at Patricia's son, causing him to be humiliated, cry and run away. He looked like he just had a serious beating, with his eyes swollen and the berry juice on his face looking like blood. Patricia was horrified, thinking the worst; Trevor told her the whole story, and then she started laughing.

"No, no, Trevor," she said. "I'm not laughing because it's funny. I'm laughing out of relief. I thought you'd been beaten up. I thought this was blood. I'm laughing because it's only berry juice."

My mom thought everything was funny. There was no subject too dark or too painful for her to tackle with humor. "Look on the bright side," she said, laughing and pointing to the half of me covered in dark berry juice. "Now you really are half black and half white."

"It's not funny!"

"Trevor, you're okay," she said. "Go and wash up. You're not hurt. You're hurt emotionally. But you're not hurt." [22]

Just half an hour later, Abel arrived home and noticed Trevor crying. At that time, Abel was still Patricia's partner and wasn't trying to be a father to Trevor, which was appreciated by Patricia's son. He was acting like a big brother, joking with Trevor and being incredibly funny. However, he could also be very mean and dangerous because he lived in the homelands, where you literally had to fight to survive. Abel had a bad temper, especially in traffic when someone would cut him off, and conflict would start. That someone barely escaped unbeaten by Abel. At this point, Patricia or Trevor didn't feel the wrath of Abel, meaning he didn't beat them. When he came home that afternoon and wanted to know what exactly happened, Patricia didn't want him involved, so she didn't want Trevor to tell him the story.

However, Trevor already knew that Abel turns into "Mr. Hyde" when he is angry. During that afternoon, he wanted the demon on his side, so he knew what to tell him. Patricia tried to calm him down (she knew this would get to him), saying it was nothing serious, just kids being kids. Abel didn't find the story very funny and asked Trevor to take him to these boys. They both went to the mulberry tree, where they found the kids playing. Trevor pointed out the ring leader, and Abel drove the car fast toward the tree and scared the kids away. They all started to run, but Abel was fast. He caught the ring leader, brought him back to the mulberry tree, stripped a tree branch, and whipped the kid hard. In the beginning, Trevor was enjoying this, but soon he realized that this was way beyond revenge, as Abel was trying to teach that kid a lesson. He was a full-grown man beating the hell out of a 12-year-old boy. Then he dragged the boy to the car and forced him to apologize to Trevor. That kid apologized, but Trevor felt like the boy was apologizing for everything he had done wrong in his life, not for the particular mulberry incident.

When they returned home, Abel and Patricia started to argue. "You can't go around hitting other people's children! You're not the law! This anger, this is no way to live!" [23] Just a few hours later, that kid's parent came by the house to confront Abel, but clearly, he didn't know what he was getting into. The parent was more of a mild, middle-aged guy who didn't stand any chance against Abel. There was no fighting, but the guy felt happy he could go back home alive, as he saw the monster in Patricia's partner.

Chapter 6:
Love Life

First Valentine's Day

In his early teenage years, Trevor wasn't at all a ladies man, as he didn't have too much luck in love affairs. He understood the concept of Valentine's Day, but only in his late teenage days would understand what it was like to be in a relationship. "The naked baby shoots you with an arrow, and you fall in love. I got that part." [24]

His first experience with Valentine's Day was the first year at H.A. Jack Primary School. He was 12 when he first understood how things worked on this special day. Trevor was confused because at the Catholic School he was not familiar with this day, as Valentine's Day was not a religious holiday. Students were selling flowers and cards, and Trevor had to ask somebody what was happening.

"What is this?" I said. "What are we doing?"

"Oh, you know," she said, "it's Valentine's Day. You pick a special person, and you tell them that you love them, and they love you back." [25]

Some of the girls in school were encouraging Trevor to ask a colored girl called Maylene to become his Valentine. "All week, the girls in school kept saying, "Who's your valentine? Who's your valentine?" I didn't know what I was supposed to do. Finally one of the girls, a white girl, said, "You should ask Maylene." The other kids agreed. "Yes, Maylene. You should definitely ask Maylene. You have to ask Maylene. You guys are *perfect* for each other." [26]

Trevor was now living in the city with his mom, his stepfather, and his baby brother, Andrew. Patricia had to sell the house in Eden Park to invest in Abel's mechanic business, but that wasn't successful, and at this point, they were living in a neighborhood called Highlands North, 30 minutes away from his school. Maylene was the only colored girl in school, and he was the only colored boy from H.A. Jack, so they had this thing in common. Every time the kids walked home, Trevor and Maylene were the last remaining kids in the group, as they lived the farthest away from school. She was cute, smart, cool, and good at tennis. Trevor liked her and enjoyed hanging out with her, but it was too early for him to be attracted to girls. The white girls were insisting on Trevor to ask her out, and Trevor was buying the girls' gossip.

"Maylene's totally got a thing for you."

"*Does* she?"

"Yeah, you guys are great together!"

"*Are* we?"

"Totally."

"Well, okay. If you say so." [27]

But he was so young and naive, as he had to be taught how love works in the early teenage years. His friends had to go t0 Maylene's friends and convince her to go out with him; Trevor didn't have the permission to talk straight to Maylene, this was a love bureaucracy rule. It was something like this: "You have your group of friends, and she has her group of friends, and your group of friends has to go to her group of friends and say, "Okay, Trevor likes Maylene. He wants her to be his valentine. We're in favor. We're ready to sign off with your approval." Her friends say, "Okay. Sounds good. We have to run it by Maylene." They go to Maylene. They consult. They tell her what they think. "Trevor says he likes you. We're in favor. We think you'd be good together. What do you say?" Maylene says, "I like Trevor." They say, "Okay. Let's move forward." They come back to us. "Maylene says she approves and she's waiting for Trevor's Valentine's Day advance."

The girls told me this process was what needed to happen. I said, "Cool.

Let's do it." The friends sorted it out, Maylene got on board, and I was all set." [28]

One week before Valentine's Day, Trevor was walking back home with Maylene, and it was an awkward silence because he was still nervous to ask her to be his Valentine. He already knew the answer, as there were serious negotiations on this matter, but still, anything could go wrong, anything could happen, and he didn't want to mess it up. He wanted to make it special. He waited until they were standing outside McDonald's, gathered all his courage, and asked her:

"Hey, Valentine's Day is coming up, and I was wondering, would you be my Valentine?"

"Yes. I'll be your Valentine." [29]

Under the golden arches, they kissed. It was Trevor's first kiss, and he felt something different that he enjoyed very much. Now he was excited about this; he had a girlfriend for the very first time in his life. He prepared for Valentine's Day, saving up his pocket money, and buying her flowers and a teddy bear. He also wrote her a poem and went to school on Valentine's Day having everything prepared (poem checked, flowers checked, teddy bear checked). He was the happiest boy in the world. Just before recess, the teacher allowed the students a period to exchange the valentines. So, he stood in front of Maylene's classroom, patiently waiting for her to show up, and watched other kids exchanging valentines. She finally came out of the classroom and walked up to Trevor, and just before he was about to wish her "Happy Valentine's Day!" she said: "Oh, hi, Trevor. Um, listen, I can't be your girlfriend anymore. Lorenzo asked me to be his valentine, and I can't have two valentines, so I'm his girlfriend now and not yours." [30]

Trevor didn't know how to react when hearing this, but he still gave the poem, flowers, and teddy bear to Maylene. She thanked him and went away. Lorenzo was a popular white guy in school, the kind of bad boy who was everything Trevor wasn't. He was the type of guy that girls would love and do his homework for him. Any of the girls dating him probably would feel like the luckiest girl alive. Trevor was devastated, but he understood why

Maylene chose Lorenzo over him. He just went back to the classroom and sat by himself until recess was over.

The Huge Crush

The situation didn't change too much in high school, as he wasn't one of the popular boys in a school of over 1000 students. He was the funny and ugly type of guy, who didn't get the attention of girls. Puberty was very harsh to him, as his face was very affected by acne. While most of the teenagers had a few pimples, he had huge blackheads and whiteheads on his face. Some people would consider that he had some allergic reaction to something. So everywhere on his forehead, cheeks, and neck, he had these ugly pustules, and this kept away most of the girls. His financial situation didn't help either, as he was poor and couldn't afford any bus to get to school, so he had to walk. This also meant that he couldn't afford a decent haircut and he had a massive Afro. Patricia was very angry with Trevor because he grew so fast and his uniforms didn't fit anymore. So, she had to buy uniforms three sizes bigger to save money. The blazer was way too big, the shoes as well, and the pants were too baggy; if he had some makeup on, Trevor would look like a clown. The year Patricia bought the uniform three sizes bigger was the year when he stopped growing, so he was stuck with this uniform, which wasn't an advantage for him when it came to attracting girls.

The heartbreak he had when he was 12 when Maylene dumped him for Lorenzo was a valuable lesson for him, as he realized that cool guys get the girls and funny guys could hang out with the cool guys and their girls. He wasn't a cool guy or a popular guy, and he knew his place in the high school yard; therefore, he didn't ask girls out, didn't have a girlfriend, and didn't even try to get one. For him, trying to get a girlfriend was to mess up the natural order of things. He was a famous nobody, as everybody knew him as the tuck shop guy, and he was welcomed everywhere because of his status. Trevor didn't belong to a specific group, but he could easily blend in with any group because he was the funny tuck shop guy, who posed no threat to anyone in the group. The moment he would become somebody, he wouldn't be welcome in most of the groups. As he was tangling with most of the groups, he knew who had a crush on a specific girl. If a cool guy had a crush on one girl, anyone attempting to get together with that girl would cause a fight. As he wasn't an alpha male, the smart thing to do was to stay on the fringe and out of trouble, not to get between a cool guy and a girl.

The only time a girl would approach Trevor was to pass a letter to a good-looking guy in the class; however, hanging out with different groups made it possible for him to become friends with some attractive girls. One was Johanna, a girl who Trevor knew from Catholic School. They went together in pre-school over there, then she moved to a different school, and then they met again at H.A. Jack Primary School. Johanna moved again to a different school and now was attending the same high school as Trevor. Because they had a common past, they somehow became friends. She was extremely popular, and her best friend could only be an even more gorgeous girl.

In many cases, a group of girls had very high standards when it came to beauty. That's why gorgeous girls stick together, and they don't let ugly ones in their group. Johanna's best friend was Zaheera, a stunning colored girl, Cape Malay, who looked like Salma Hayek. Johanna was the kind of girl who would go out and was all about kissing guys, and they were into her. On the other hand, Zaheera was extremely shy, and despite being so hot, not many guys were after her. Both of them were a grade lower than him, but they were amongst the most popular girls in school. Trevor didn't dare to date girls, mostly because of his looks and financial situation, but this didn't mean that he couldn't talk to them. They were also humans, and humans love to laugh, and he was the right guy to make them laugh. Trevor accepted his status of the funny and non-threatening guy, the guy everyone likes to have around. He had the biggest crush on Zaheera, but he never felt worthy of her. They would hang out and have great conversations together. He was her confidant, a trusting and reliable friend, but never her lover. Trevor decided to play it slow to win the heart of Zaheera, so he developed a strategy to get her. He was planning to go together with her at the matric dance, but that was three years away. It was like all the clichés from the American high school movies when the hot girl would date all the jocks and jerks, but eventually would end up with the geeky but super-friendly guy who had a crush on her since kindergarten but never dared to tell her what he felt.

Trevor was planning to get closer to her, so she could discuss with him every little secret that she had. He wouldn't prevent her from going out with other boys, as it was natural for a gorgeous girl to go on dates. When she was set up on a date with a guy named Gary, she told Trevor everything about the date, including the fact that she didn't like Gary at all, but it was an arranged date through the love bureaucracy. Gary was a shy guy from the popular group, and she was just a stunning girl (but also shy) in a popular group. They needed a person, or a whole group, to liaise with them and to arrange their date. One day, Trevor gathered his courage to ask for her phone number, and he was surprised when she offered him the phone number. To play it cool, he didn't call her immediately after arriving at home, but he called instead in the evening. They spoke for probably an hour, but this marked the beginning of a special period in their friendship because they started talking more at school and over the phone. Trevor never made a move on her; he never manned-up to tell her what he felt because he was too scared.

Zaheera's relationship with Gary was an ongoing break-up and get back together thing, but at one point they broke up for good. This was excellent news for Trevor, and he was seeing his master plan working, and there were only two and a half years left until the matric dance. However, things would dramatically change after the mid-year school holidays; Zaheera didn't come back to school, and Trevor asked Johanna about Zaheera.

"Hey, where's Zaheera?" I said. "She hasn't been around for a while. Is she sick?"

"No," she said. "Didn't anyone tell you? She left the school. She doesn't go here anymore."

"What?"

"Yeah, she left."

My first thought was, " *Wow, okay. That's news. I should give her a call to catch up.*"

"What school did she move to?" I asked.

"She didn't. Her dad got a job in America. During the break, they moved there. They've emigrated."

"What?"

"Yeah. She's gone. She was such a good friend, too. I'm really sad. Are you as sad as I am?"

"Uh…yeah," I said, still trying to process everything. "I liked Zaheera. She was really cool."

"Yeah, she was super sad, too, because she had such a huge crush on you. She was always waiting for you to ask her out. Okay, I gotta go to class! Bye!" [31]

Johanna took off, leaving Trevor speechless; he couldn't believe what she just told him. It was too much information to handle; first that she was gone, second that she moved to America (so she was gone for good), and most of all that she always liked him. The news gave him a devastating blow, and now he was rewinding in his mind all the time they spent together and countless hours of conversations over the phone or face to face, realizing that he had numerous occasions to tell her what he felt and to ask her to be his girlfriend. Trevor couldn't help asking himself, "what if I asked her out?" It was just a few words that he never said to her, (never dared to say what he felt toward her) which could have changed his life. Now she was gone to a different country, far away from him.

Matric Dance

During high school, Trevor developed his entrepreneurial skills. It started with the tuck shop run when he would make some pocket money, but as he was growing up, he discovered another way to make a handsome income. The food-run business had evolved into something a lot more complex: selling pirated CDs he made at home. As frugal as Patricia was, he still convinced her to buy him a PC, telling her it's something he needed for school. She bought the computer, which created an interesting opportunity for Trevor. He also had an internet connection and a CD writer offered as a gift by a friend at school. The computer was his world, as he didn't consider dating any girl—the only ones where the naked ones from his computer.

It was Trevor's senior year with the matric dance approaching quickly, and he was facing the same Valentine's Day dilemma he previously had. However, this time he was prepared and had some "aces up his sleeve." During high-school, Trevor learned that cool guys get the girls and funny guys like him can hang out with the cool guys and their girls. Money was no longer becoming a problem for him, as business was going better than ever, and he was getting an income higher than some of the salaries in South Africa, just by selling pirated CDs. Having a computer with an internet connection was not a common thing back then, so he was privileged.

On top of that, he had the CD writer, which generated his business. He had a hard drive full of the most popular music, all tracks were downloaded from the internet, and he used the CD writer to burn CDs and to sell them to people. The prize was unbeatable, cheaper than the one from a store, but there wasn't any difference in quality. His business would not be so successful without the help of his middlemen, Bongani and Tom, who would sell his CDs on different markets in exchange for a cut.

Tom was a natural-born salesman (and a liar), a true hustler, and the kind of guy who would always work an angle to try to cut a deal. He was the same grade as Trevor, but he was studying at a government school in Northview, which was a proper ghetto school. That was his selling territory. On one occasion, Trevor went with Tom to a place called Hammanskraal to see a talent show. Having two frugal parents, Trevor was not a big spender at all. Although business was going well, he didn't invest the money he made on expensive clothing. He did have a pair of Timberland boots, which were the only decent piece of clothing he had. He was among the few in South Africa to own a pair of Timberland boots. When they left for the talent show, Tom asked him to make sure he was wearing the expensive boots. The talent show was in a hall in the middle of nowhere, but the place was full of people, and Tom knew almost everyone in there, as he was shaking hands and chatting with most of the people there. The talent show consisted of poetry, singing, and dancing. Suddenly, the host was on the stage announcing the main event of the evening:

"We've got a special performer, a rapper all the way from America. Please welcome…Spliff Star!"

Spliff Star was Busta Rhymes' hype man at the time. I sat there, confused. *What? Spliff Star? In Hammanskraal?*

Then everyone in the room turned and looked at me. Tom walked over and whispered in my ear.

Dude, come up on stage."

"What?"

"Come on stage."

"Dude, what are you talking about?"

"Dude, please, you're gonna get me in so much shit. They've already paid me the money."

"*Money?* What money?"

Of course, what Tom had failed to tell me was that he'd told these people he was bringing a famous rapper from America to come and rap in their talent show. He had demanded to be paid up front for doing so, and I, in my Timberlands, was that famous American rapper.

"Screw you," I said. "I'm not going anywhere."

"Please, dude, I'm begging you. Please do me this favor. Please. There's this girl here, and I wanna get with her, and I told her I know all these rappers…Please. I'm begging you."

"Dude, I'm not Spliff Star. What am I gonna do?!"

"Just rap Busta Rhymes songs."

"But I don't know any of the lyrics."

"It doesn't matter. These people don't speak English." [32]

They improvised on the spot, so Tom did a horrible beatbox and Trevor just spit some Busta Rhymes lyrics, and the crowd cheered and applauded. They thought they had in front of them a real American rapper, spitting out lyrics in his Timberland boots.

Trevor helped Tom get together with that girl by doing this talent show in the middle of nowhere. However, Tom returned the favor and promised to hook him up with a gorgeous girl for the matric dance (the equivalent of the American prom), as it was just two months away, and Trevor was still without a date. Tom was determined to set up Trevor with a date for this event in exchange for a better cut of the CDs he was selling.

"I can get you a girl to go with you to the dance," he said.

"No, you can't."

"Yes, I can. Let's make a deal."

"I don't want one of your deals, Tom."

"No, listen, here's the deal. If you give me a better cut on the CDs I'm selling, plus a bunch of free music for myself, I'll come back with the most beautiful girl you've ever seen in your life, and she'll be your date for the dance."

"Okay, I'll take that deal because it's never going to happen."

"Do we have a deal?"

"We have a deal, but it's not going to happen."

"But do we have a *deal*?"

"It's a deal."

"Okay, I'm going to find you a date. She's going to be the most beautiful girl you've ever seen, and you're going to take her to the matric dance, and you're going to be a superstar." [33]

Tom was considered a con-man, but he was one of the ones, as he would always deliver something and wouldn't leave you empty-handed. When he was following his interest, he would show commitment, and this case made no difference. Trevor quickly forgot about the deal Tom promised him, as he didn't take him seriously. However, Tom came to Trevor one day claiming that he had found the girl for him. They both went into the city to meet her, and when Trevor met her, he was just stupefied. The girl Tom set him up with was a gorgeous black girl, with Pedi heritage (a smaller African tribe). Her name was Babiki, and she was part of a poor black family, but they were always dressing fashionably and acted rich. Every time Trevor and Babiki went on a date, they were never alone; as they were double dating (Tom was with them all the time). Tom was the entertainer of the group, making everyone loosen up and have a great time. She was extremely shy, and he was very nervous. Babiki was hugging Trevor every time they said "goodbye," but one time she kissed him. He was just in Heaven, as he finally had a girlfriend just in time for the dance.

Now that the girl was secured, Trevor also had to prepare for this event because he had always pictured it like in the American movies, with limousines, a great time, and loss of virginity. His stepfather always had plenty of cars at his disposal, being a mechanic, but Trevor had one particular car in mind: Abel's BMW. That was Abel's favorite car, his prized jewel, but unfortunately for Trevor, he wouldn't let anyone else drive it. One day, Trevor was hanging out with Tom at Abel's garage, and Tom was talking about Trevor's date. Since he realized the importance of this event, Abel was feeling generous and was determined to help Trevor on this occasion. He offered him the Mazda, but Patricia's son wanted to make a great impression, so he needed the BMW.

Tom stepped in and worked his magic.

"Bra Abie," he said. "I don't think you understand. If you saw the girl Trevor is taking to the dance, you would see why this is so important. Let's make a deal. If we bring her here and she's the most beautiful girl you've ever seen in your life, you'll let him take the BMW."

Abel thought about it.

"Okay. Deal." [34]

Trevor went with Tom to get Babiki, and then they presented her to Abel:

"Abel, this is Babiki. Babiki, this is Abel."

Abel smiled big, charming as always.

"Nice to meet you," he said.

They chatted for a few minutes. Tom and Babiki left. Abel turned to me.

"Is that the girl?"

"Yes."

"You can take the BMW." [35]

Trevor's sense of fashion was limited to a brand of clothing called Powerhouse, which was the kind of clothes weightlifter would wear. This brand stood for what Trevor believed in and loved. He was just another teenager with no friends, who loved dogs and thought muscles were cool. He just loved it, as he had the same outfit in five different colors. His other middleman, Bongani, found out about Trevor's date and offered to help him improve his looks. He noticed that Trevor had a fashion problem and was willing to help him, but to do that they would need to go shopping. Realizing that he needed more money, Trevor begged his mother to give him money to buy an outfit for the matric dance. Frugal Patricia was finally convinced and gave Trevor 2,000 rand for one outfit. This was the largest amount of money she gave Trevor. It wasn't much, but Bongani thought they could still make it work with this budget. Just like Babiki's family, Trevor had to look rich, although he was poor. Bongani gave him the golden advice of shopping, to buy one expensive clothing item and the rest of the clothing has to be cheap, good-looking, and quality. The expensive item would catch the eye of others, and they would not realize that the other stuff you wear is basic.

A character Trevor always admired was Neo from *The Matrix*; he loved the way he dressed and the way he moved. He found many similarities with Neo; he was a just another nerd, completely useless at almost everything, but in secret, he was a superhero. It looked like Trevor only needed a bald black guy to step into his life and to show him the path to awesomeness. Bongani was playing the role of Morpheus, and he was determined to help Trevor look sharp, the kind of guy his date would find irresistible. They went shopping together and spent 1,200 rands on something which Trevor thought was very cool (thanks to Neo). It was a leather jacket, very similar to the one Neo had in *The Matrix*, and they completed the outfit with some suede shoes, simple black pants, and a cream-white sweater. Once the outfit problem was resolved, they had to focus on Trevor's haircut. He had a huge Afro, which was very difficult to comb.

Bongani was from Alexandra, a proper black ghetto which was very similar to Soweto, the township where Trevor would visit his grandmother. There were plenty of hair salons in Alexandra, so they went in these salons to do something regarding Trevor's hair. The girls at the hair salon suggested cornrowing his hair, but it had to be relaxed first. In a salon, the hair stylist helped Trevor relax his hair, and they went to a different salon to cornrow it. Trevor felt like in the TV shows, where they take a dorky guy and give him an extreme makeover, starting with his clothes and finishing up with his hairstyle. He was a completely different young man; the hair was looking very slick, his face was a lot cleaner than a few years before, as now the pustules turned into simple pimples and his face was a lot clearer. Everyone appreciated his new look, even his mother, although she would tease him.

"Oooooh! They turned my baby boy into a pretty little girl! I've got a little girl! You're so pretty!"

"Mom! C'mon. Stop it."

"Is this the way you're telling me that you're gay?"

"What? No. Why would you say that?"

"You know it's okay if you are."

"No, Mom. I'm not gay." [36]

It was the night of the matric dance when Tom came over to help Trevor get ready. Just like a girl before going on a date, Trevor prepared intensively, the only difference was that he didn't wear makeup. Everything looked perfect, the hair and the clothes, it was only one thing missing: the keys to Abel's BMW. Since it was a Saturday night, Abel did what he always did, started drinking with his workers and by the time Trevor and Tom came to pick up the keys, he was completely wasted. He didn't want to hand over the keys, tricking the boys into buying him first a few cases of beer before handing over the keys. When they arrived with the beers, surprise, Abel did not intend to let Trevor drive his car. He claimed that he needed the car tonight and offered in exchange the keys to the Mazda. Trevor and Tom sat over there for almost half an hour trying to convince Abel to keep his promise, but they couldn't reason with him as he was completely drunk. Eventually, they took the Mazda and went to Babiki's house to pick her up. It was already one hour late, and she was pissed off. Tom went in and convinced her to go to the dance, so Trevor and Babiki went on their first date together alone.

The matric dance was not held at the school, as the school didn't have such a place to host festive events. It was held at a different location, a place Trevor was not aware of. Babiki was wearing a red dress and looked smoking hot, but she wasn't in a good mood. He smiled at her, told her how beautiful she was, and went to the dance. The happy event was held at a venue in a different part of the city, a part which Trevor was not very familiar with. He was always on his cell phone asking for guidance from some of his friends to get there and eventually got lost. He drove for more than an hour in the dark, whilst Babiki sat in the passenger seat completely silent and didn't say anything to Trevor. He was completely lost, and she was having the worst date of her life. They arrived at the venue two hours late, Trevor parked the car and gallantly opened the door for her, but she didn't want to get out of the car.

"Are you ready?" I said. "Let's go in."

"No."

"No? What…what do you mean, 'no'?"

"No."

"Okay…but why?"

"No."

"But we need to go inside. The dance is inside."

"No." [37]

After 20 minutes of failed attempts to get her out of the car, Trevor went inside looking for Bongani, telling him that his date wouldn't come out of the car. Bongani went back with Trevor to the parking lot to convince Babiki to join the dance, and his jaw just dropped when he saw Babiki. She was the most beautiful girl he had ever seen and immediately went back inside to call the other guys. Soon 20 other guys came to the parking lot, and Babiki was like the main attraction at the zoo; everybody wanted to take pictures with her. Babiki was not in the mood for this, a shy girl like her didn't want that much attention. Trevor stood petrified, watching the most important date of his life becoming a circus, a spectacle bigger than the matric dance itself. No one believed Trevor was dating such a hot girl, so they all had to come into the parking lot and check her out. Since the date was ruined anyway, Trevor started to drink from a bottle of brandy smuggled from the venue by a friend of his. Bongani tried a last attempt to convince the girl to join the party, but after his attempt, he had a confused look.

"Yo, Trevor," he said, "your date does not speak English."

"What?"

"Your date. She does not speak any English."

"That's not possible."

I got up and walked over to the car. I asked her a question in English, and she gave me a blank stare.

Bongani looked at me.

"How did you not know that your date does not speak English?"

"I...I don't know."

"Have you never spoken to her?"

"Of course I have—or, wait...*have* I?" [38]

Soon he realized that every time they had a conversation was through Tom or Babiki's older sister, who all spoke English, but Babiki couldn't. Any other conversation at his dates with her was in Pedi or Sotho, languages which Trevor didn't understand, but this was something normal in South Africa and didn't bother him at that time. He now just realized that the only language Babiki could fluently speak was Pedi, a very rare language that many black people didn't know. Tom never mentioned anything about her flaw, although he knew it, he just wanted to get a better deal for himself out of selling the CDs compiled by Trevor. He was dating this gorgeous girl for more than a month, and they didn't have a single conversation together, just the normal "Hi" or "Bye."

Trevor had one theory regarding Babiki. He thought she never wanted to go to the matric dance with him in the first place, but she probably owed something to Tom, so she did him this favor. If you think that Tom could convince anyone to do anything, this was an option.

By this point, Trevor became desperate as he used his hands to gesticulate and to communicate with her. They still couldn't talk to each other and Trevor asked around if anyone spoke Pedi, but nobody over there spoke Pedi. The special night was pretty much compromised, and Trevor didn't go to the matric dance. When the night was over, he drove Babiki back to her home. Even though she had such an attitude toward him, Trevor was still trying to be a gentleman and properly end this night. Then, out of nowhere, Babiki gave him a proper kiss, a gesture which left Trevor very confused. He opened her door very gallantly, and as she was heading toward her apartment, she turned for the last time and wave to him for the last time.

Chapter 7:
A Booming Business

Pirated CDs

Trevor's friendly attitude made him the perfect guy for the tuck shop guy position. He was very social, open-minded, and got along with mostly everybody, regardless of their group. He was also the fastest guy in school, a true "Springbok." Sandringham School was the perfect place for racial diversity. It had black kids, colored kids, white kids, but also Indian and Chinese kids.

In many cases, the kids were using just the nicknames instead of the real names. For example, there was a Chinese kid who looked like Bolo Yeung from Jean-Claude Van Damme's movie, *Bloodsport*, so naturally, his nickname was Bolo. Another Chinese guy was named Bruce Lee (exactly like the famous movie star), which everyone over there thought was very cool. Bolo was one of Trevor's clients, so Trevor was doing the food-run for him on plenty of occasions. He was also famous for pirating PlayStation video games, as kids gave him their console and Bolo would return the PlayStation to them with a chip inside, which enabled them to play pirated games. He was a friend of Andrew, a white geek who was in the business of pirated CDs.

One day they were discussing black kids getting their merchandise, as they were the kind that sometimes didn't pay. Andrew and Bolo were both afraid of asking the black kids to pay. Trevor overheard their conversation and suggested an alternative. "Listen, you shouldn't get upset. Black people don't have any money, so trying to get more stuff for less money is just what we do. But let me help. I'll be your middleman. You give me the merchandise, and I'll sell it, and then I'll handle getting the money. In return, you give me a cut of the sale." [39] Andrew and Bolo agreed, and Trevor started a collaboration with them. As he was the tuck shop guy, he already had connections, so already had potential buyers. He made some pocket cash through this collaboration and was able to bet the best components for his computer. Andrew told him some tips about cheap but quality parts, how to assemble or repair them, and also showed Trevor how his business worked.

The only thing Trevor was missing was the CD writer, which was the most expensive part you can add to a computer and cost at least 2,000 rands. Trevor was the middleman for Bolo and Andrew for about a year until Bolo left school. There were some nasty rumors that his parents were arrested, but no one knew what happened. Andrew was also two years older than Trevor, and he was about to get matriculated, so he made an unexpected and valuable gift. He handed over to Trevor his CD writer as an appreciation for his collaboration. At that time, only a few black kids owned a computer, but to have a CD writer to it was just something unbelievable. The selling market was already made. Trevor only had to continue the legacy of Andrew and Bolo. He was selling one CD with 30 rands when in stores the original one was between 100 and 150 rands. He had instant success and money was coming his way. Although it seems like the instinct for business was in his DNA, he didn't know much about music, as Christian music from church didn't count. The CD writer he received was burning CDs at 1x speed, which meant he could only copy CDs at the same speed as he would listen to the songs. After arriving home from school, Trevor would spend at least five to six hours in his room to copy CDs. He already built up his speaker system, using some forgotten speakers from Abel's old cars. He just sat in the room while the music played and the CDs were copying, but sometimes he wouldn't listen to the music, as he was living by a dealer code: "Never get high on your own supply." [40]

Having internet access meant he could get access to all kind of music, from rock to hip-hop. South African music was appreciated, but the most successful genre was American hip hop and R&B. DMX, Jagged Edge, and Montell Jordan were popular; you name it, Trevor had it. He also wanted to grow his business, so he invested in it. He increased his internet speed from a dial-up connection with a 24K modem to a 56K one, and bought the best CD writers he could find in South Africa. Copying CDs was a very time-consuming task, so he couldn't sell the discs and write them at the same time. He needed his very own middlemen to expand his operation. His friend Tom was the salesperson for Northview, while Bongani, another friend, was the salesman for Alexandra.

Business was growing rapidly, as both of his middlemen were selling plenty of CDs. Trevor was copying discs with songs from the same artist, just like an album. One day, Bongani suggested compiling a CD with tracks from different albums or different artists. In the store when you buy the album of an artist just for a few famous songs you already knew and mostly skipped other tracks. So why not create a compilation with the best songs, so you don't have to skip any song? Trevor thought this was a great idea, so he started mixing some tracks and copied them on discs. These kinds of CDs became bestsellers, so Bongani had another good suggestion. "Can you make the tracks fade into one another so the music moves from track one to track two without a break and the beat carries on? It'll be like a DJ playing a complete set the whole night." [41]

Trevor downloaded software called BPM "beats per minute," which had a very cool interface, showing two vinyl records, just like an old-school DJ desk. The software allowed him to mix and fade between songs, with very nice sound effects, doing what a DJ could do live. He made some party CDs, which were selling incredibly well. Business was booming, and by the time of the matric dance, Trevor was making around 500 rands a week, which was a very decent income, considering that there are maids in South Africa who are paid less today. It wasn't a fortune, but for a teenager with no expenses, this was a dream income. Getting all this money meant that he was able to afford to eat out in places like McDonald's or KFC. For an American, eating at these fast-food chains was probably something ordinary, but for people in South Africa, this was a mania. Everyone was just crazy for all these fast-food chains. White people were mostly into Burger King, while black people mostly enjoyed McDonald's and KFC. At the end of apartheid, the people of South Africa were finally free, but with the freedom also came McDonald's. For them, a McDonald's fast-food restaurant was the symbol of freedom. Trevor's family couldn't afford to eat over there, but now that he had this extra income, Trevor could finally afford to eat over there. Such a restaurant opened just two blocks away from him, so he didn't have to walk too much to get a proper fast-food meal. McDonald's in South Africa didn't have the supersize meals, so Trevor had to order the large number one meal. He fell in love with McDonald's from the first bite, but as he was eating his burger, he realized that it was not that good. However, it was good enough to cause addiction because as soon as you finished it, you couldn't wait to get back the following day to try another one. It left him wanting more, and once he had this taste, homemade dinner wasn't very appealing to him.

"Tonight we're having chicken livers."

"No, I'm gonna have McDonald's."

"Tonight we're having dog bones."

"I think I'm gonna go with McDonald's again."

"Tonight we're having chicken feet."

"Hmmmmm…Okay, I'm in. But tomorrow I'm eating McDonald's." [42]

Like a true businessman, Trevor also bought a cell phone, a cordless device which had a good enough range to speak on the phone all over to McDonald's and back, with the base placed just outside his window. These were the good days, the lush life, but none of it would be possible without Andrew and his valuable gift. He was Trevor's mentor, the person who introduced him to the secrets of CD piracy and who also taught him the best-kept secrets of the music piracy and computer functionality. It's said: "Give a man a fish, and you feed him for a day. Teach him how to fish, and you feed him for a lifetime." However, it wasn't that easy to catch a fish just with bare hands; humans would need to have the proper tools to get the fish. Trevor was a natural-born salesman, but without the knowledge and resources, what he received from Andrew wouldn't make it in the music piracy world.

DJ-ing and the Dance Crew

One day when Trevor was copying party CDs, Bongani just dropped by to take his inventory and noticed Trevor's skills as a DJ when he was mixing songs in his computer. He was intrigued and was wondering if Trevor was doing this live. Trevor confirmed that everything was live, so Bongani had the idea of live mixing in front of a crowd. He was from Alexandra, a proper black ghetto, famous for its parties and murders, so he saw an opportunity in what Trevor was doing. Parties in Alexandra were wild; they were the best thing about that place. There wasn't any official invitation, as everything was happening spontaneously. You didn't need a permit to throw a party over there; if you had a tent, you could throw a party on your street, blocking the intersection and when drivers showed up, they would make a U-turn, and nobody would get upset. The only rule was if you were throwing a party in front of somebody's house that somebody could easily join the party and share the alcohol.

Back then, a DJ could mix for a few hours, according to the number of vinyl records he had. Usually, parties were taking all night, so the presence of several DJs was required. Trevor had instead a hard disk packed with tons of music, which got Bongani excited.

"How much music do you have?" he asked.

"Winamp says I can play for a week."

"We'll make a fortune." [43]

Their first gig was the New Year's Eve party in Alexandra, the year they graduated from Sandringham High School. Bogani and Trevor gathered the necessary equipment (Trevor's tower of speakers, the screen, computer, mouse, keyboard, and all the cables. They took a mini-bus to Alexandra and installed all the equipment in front of Bongani's house. They took electricity from inside the house, borrowed a tent, set up, and people just came from all over the "hood." Their party was a massive success, the biggest in Alexandra at that New Year's Eve and this was no joke. The whole street was full from one end to the other. Word got out, and people in

Alexandra were talking about a light-skinned boy playing music from a computer. The party lasted till dawn and Trevor, Bongani, and all his friends ended up exhausted and wasted on the front lawn of Bongani's house. They made such an impression that they were booked for different parties in Alexandra.

Fast internet connection created a great advantage for Trevor, as he had access to exclusive tracks so fresh, most people hadn't heard of them yet. The vibe was so fresh that many people could feel the rhythm, but didn't know how to dance to such music. They were aware that the DJ-ing activity needed a different kind of advertisement. This is how they came with the idea of having their very own dance group. Since their crew from the "hood" already knew all the songs, they were the perfect candidates to become a part of this group. The crew was formed of Bongani, the ring leader, the person who brought everyone together and got things moving. Then there was Mzi, a close friend of Bongani, Bheki—the person who could always find you alcohol—Kakoatse (aka G or Mr. Nice Guy), who was only interested in girls, and their best dancer, Hitler.

The way people name their newborn babies is a bit strange in South Africa, as they always select a name which means something to them. However, ever since the white man set foot on South African soil, black people from here were required to have a European name as well, so the white people can pronounce it. Take for instance Patricia Nombuyiselo Noah; Patricia was her European name, Nombuyiselo was her African name. Those European names could be picked randomly, straight from the Bible, or after Hollywood celebrities, but also politicians. Therefore, you could meet people in South Africa named Napoleon, Mussolini, and Hitler. Black people were not educated and didn't have any general knowledge about history. That's why they weren't aware of dictators and what they have done. For old black people, Hitler was a tank helping Germany win the war. Others had heard of a guy called Hitler who was causing the Allies to lose the war. This was a name considered to represent something powerful; it was the kind of name which was suitable for a vicious dog in South Africa.

Being a Sandringham student, Trevor was taught just a few basic details about Hitler and wasn't taught to think critically about him and his actions, and also wasn't taught that apartheid was based on his sick ideas. He was only taught simple facts, that Hitler invaded Poland in 1939 and the Soviet Union in 1941, but no details regarding the Holocaust and the genocide of other people. Black people would surely resent this name if they only knew that this character was the inspiration of apartheid. They weren't taught that Hitler sentenced to death six million Jews, just like Europeans were not taught of the atrocities done by Belgium and Portugal in Congo and Angola; how many black people were killed directly by guns; or in the gold and diamond mines. If all over Europe and North America he was one of the most evil leaders, in South Africa he was seen as a strong leader from the history books. This is probably how the most talented dancer from their crew got his name.

In the hood, there was another way to become popular and get girls, not just if you had fine clothes and cars. If you were poor, then dancing was the secret to become popular. Once the dance crew was formed, the crew competed against other dancers in a few competitions. Every crew brought their best dancers, Trevor and Bongani had Hitler, and there wasn't anyone better than him. The way he moved and the way he looked made the crowd wild. Just like in the American dance movies, Hitler was the one to "serve" anyone. When there was such a competition, the dancers came to the stage and did a couple of numbers, but Hitler was kept for the "grand finale." He was the perfect one to humiliate all the best dancers from the hood, but his moves were the result of long and intensive practices. Every morning he would train, cranking the volume of his stereo and exercising his moves to house and hip-hop music. At parties, Trevor was the official DJ of the crew. He cranked up the volume and started preparing the crowd.

"Are you ready?! I can't hear you! Let me hear you make some noise!" People would start screaming, and Hitler would jump into the middle of the semicircle, and the crowd would lose it. Hitler would do his thing while the guys circled him, shouting him on. *"Go Hit-ler! Go Hit-ler! Go Hit-ler! Go Hit-ler!"* And because this was hip-hop, the crew would do that thing where you shoot your arm out in front of you with your palm flat, bopping it up and down to the beat. *"Go Hit-ler! Go Hit-ler! Go Hit-ler! Go Hit-ler!"* We'd have the whole crowd in a frenzy, a thousand people in the street chanting

along with their hands in the air. *"Go Hit-ler! Go Hit-ler! Go Hit-ler! Go Hit-ler!"* [44]

The official stage name of the crew was the "Black and White Boys," while the dancers were called the "Springbok Boys." They soon started to become quite famous, being booked at parties all over the area. They were playing at parties organized by successful black families, with people who would love to have a proper block party. They were so famous that they received invitations from white people who wanted them at their parties. This is how they were invited to perform at different events called "diversity programs." These were a few of activities held all across South Africa having the purpose of embracing and learning the culture of different cultures.

The crew was invited to perform at a Jewish school called King David School, in such a "diversity program." Once they got there, they saw representations of Greek and flamenco dancers, traditional Zulu musicians, and many other acts. In the crowd, there were only Jewish kids with yarmulkes, all ready to have a great time. Trevor made a very nice atmosphere; everyone was having fun, the crowd was just electrified, until the main protagonist came to the stage, on Redman's "Let's Get Dirty."

"I started the song, the dancers fanned out in their semicircle, and I got on the mic.

"Are you guys ready?!"

"Yeahhhhhh!"

"You guys are not ready! Are you *ready*?!"

"Yeeeaaahhhhhhhh!"

"All right! Give it up and make some noise for *HIIIIIITTTTTLLLLLEERRRRRRRRRRR!!!"*

Hitler jumped out to the middle of the circle and started killing it. The guys around him were all chanting, *"Go Hit-ler! Go Hit-ler! Go Hit-ler! Go Hit-ler!"* They had their arms out in front of them bouncing to the rhythm. *"Go Hit-ler! Go Hit-ler! Go Hit-ler! Go Hit-ler!"* And I was right there on the mic leading them along. *"Go Hit-ler! Go Hit-ler! Go Hit-ler! Go Hit-ler!"* [45] (C:\Users\Farhan\Downloads\Order 1479 - Trevor Noah - Final (1) EDITED.docx#a__ftn45)

Suddenly everyone in the crowd stopped, and every Jew in the hall was stupefied. All the teachers, parents, and chaperones just froze and watched horrified the spectacle displayed by Trevor's crew, until a teacher unplugged the system to stop the madness going on stage. The teacher was just outraged. "How *dare* you?! This is disgusting! You horrible, disgusting, vile creature! How *dare* you?!" Trevor didn't understand the teacher's frustration.

"Lady," I said, "I think you need to calm down."

"I will *not* calm down! How dare you come here and insult us?!"

"This is not insulting anyone. This is who we are!"

"Get out of here! You people are disgusting." [46]

Trevor was getting pissed off right now, being convinced that this lady was racist.

"Listen, lady. We're free now. We're gonna do what we're gonna do. You can't stop us."

"I'll have you know that my people stopped people like you before, and we can stop you again." [47]

She was referring, of course, to the Jewish people stopping the Nazis of World War II, but this is not what Trevor had in mind. "All I was hearing was some white lady shouting about how white people beat us before, and they'll beat us again."

I said, "You will *never* stop us again, lady"—and here's where I played the trump card—"You'll never stop us because now we have *Nelson Mandela* on our side! And he *told* us we can do this!"

"What?!" [48]

Money Lending

After he finished school, Trevor spent most of his free time in Alexandra, one of the toughest places to be in the Johannesburg area. With his friend Bongani, he founded the Black and White Boys, a very popular crew which performed at many parties in the hood. Bongani was most likely Trevor's best friend, and they got close, ever since they started the collaboration on selling pirated CDs. However, this wasn't the only profitable activity they had, as DJ-ing and the dance crew was an important part of their life. Bongani could bring up the best in each person; he just was the best motivator. Trevor got close to him because he saw the potential in him that no one else could see. He used to be a skinny guy until he started working out, following the strict rules discovered in a bodybuilding magazine. He then became buff and a guy who imposed respect, but he didn't receive a reputation of a tough guy until he beat up one of the most feared bullies at school. Trevor enjoyed spending time in Alexandra, as he finally found a group of friends who accepted him as he was: a friendly light-skin dude. If rich white guys just wanted to spend a gap year in Europe traveling, immediately after graduating, Trevor's gap year was spent in Alexandra, a place which was nicknamed Gomorrah. During apartheid, living in townships like Alexandra and Soweto was not something to be proud of, but the fall of this regime also brought the black American influence over South Africa. Suddenly, it was very cool to live in ghettos, just like in the American movies "Boys n the Hood," "Menace II Society," and many others. Teenagers growing up in these ghettos were now proud of their identity.

Trevor missed the vibe specific to the townships, something he noticed from his childhood in Soweto. That's probably why he was curious to check how the ghetto evolved after the fall of apartheid. Bongani introduced Trevor to Alexandra, and although this was a dangerous place, having gangsters being chased by police, helicopters flying around, gun battles, Trevor never got in trouble over there. Bongani was one of the guys from the hood who didn't do anything illegal, besides selling pirated CDs, of course. Growing up in such times, this activity was not considered a felony.

They were living the dream and making a decent income through music piracy activity and also DJ-ing and dancing. This fact allowed them to have a better financial situation than most of the people from the hood. Trevor started hanging out with the crew in Alexandra when he was 17, immediately after graduating from Sandringham High School. His stepfather's abusive behavior made him spend most of his time away from home, but also the fact that he was planning to go to university and then become a computer programmer. However, this plan required money for tuition and other costs, and he didn't have the money at the moment. He was determined to make as much money as possible with copying CDs, DJ-ing, and being the host for the dance crew. All his equipment was moved to Bongani's garage, so that's where he copied his CDs and spent his days.

Amongst the most faithful customers Trevor had, were the mini-bus drivers, who were always looking for the latest music because new music always attracted more customers for them. They placed the order in the morning, went on their regular route, and came back a few hours later to pick up their order. Food was extremely cheap in the ghetto because you were able to get a decent meal for only two rands. If you wanted some upgrades, you had to pay extra. Over there, the biggest arrogance was to add cheese to the meal, since cheese was very expensive. They had money to spend and were not afraid to show it. If you had a hamburger in the hood that was a great thing, but if you had a cheeseburger that meant automatically you had more money than the guy with the burger. That's why there was the expression "cheese boy" as a reference to the people who had more money than most of the people in the hood.

The fall of apartheid brought freedom to South Africa, but also brought an increased unemployment rate. During that regime, mostly everyone was busy (although remuneration was extremely low), but after its fall, the cost of labor increased and along with it the unemployment rate. The people living in ghettos were not very sure of their jobs, teenagers were waking up every morning, their parents were going to work or not, and then they just went to sit on the curve all day, talking nonsense. This is how life was for the regular teenager in Alexandra or any other hood. Most of them had modest education, so getting a decent job was out of the question, as their best hope at a job was to work in retail. Felony and other criminal activity was part of everyone's life in the hood, it only depended on the level of it, from hardcore gangsters selling drugs or weapons, to the desperate mom buying food which fell from the back of a truck. Trevor and the gang criminal activity consisted of the pirated CDs business. Every day, he took an extender and played the music outside, people stopped by and ordered some music. But they never considered this activity as illegal, "if copying CDs is wrong, why would they make CD writers?" [49] Trevor probably owed all these artists tons of money, but he didn't feel guilty at all.

Nobody had money to pay for the CDs on the spot, so Bongani saw an opportunity in this. Just like Tom, he was also a hustler, but he had a bigger picture and worked out deals which were profitable for them. If a mini-bus driver came to order something and didn't have to pay because he just started the shift, they would make a deal to pay at the end of the shift or of the week, charging a bit of interest. Bongani had a great idea on how to make more money, lending money to people in need. Cash was the most precious thing you could have in the hood, and they had plenty thanks to the pirated CD business. Word got out, and people were coming to them for short-term loans. They were offering a guy 100 rands, and the guy would pay back at the end of the week 120 rands. Money was multiplying, and they built up a strong reputation in the hood. Bongani also found other money-making opportunities. There is a common place where people would sell all kinds of stuff, from VCR to TV sets. Nobody asked where the product was from, and the prices were unbeatable. Normally, drug addicts were the guys selling this merchandise, which was usually stolen, but they wanted the cash fast to get rid of it until they get caught. If a guy were negotiating with a drug addict to buy a DVD player and the seller would ask too much, Bongani would step in and work his magic.

"Look, I understand you can't pay for the DVD player now," Bongani says. "But how much are you willing to pay for it?"

"I'll pay 120," he says.

"Okay, cool."

Then Bongani takes the crackhead aside.

"How much do you want for the DVD player?"

"I want 140."

"Okay, listen. You're a crackhead. This is a stolen DVD player. I'm going to give you 50."

The crackhead protests a bit, but then he takes the money because he's a crackhead and it's cash, and crack is all about the now. Then, Bongani goes back to the working guy.

"All right. We'll do 120. Here's your DVD player. It's yours."

"But I don't have the 120."

"It's cool. You can take it now, only instead of 120 you give us 140 when you get your wages."

"Okay." [50]

In plain mathematics, with an investment of 50 rands, they just made 140 rands. If Bongani knows that the working guy works for instance at the Nike store, he can get an even better deal.

"How much do you pay for a pair of Nikes with your staff discount?" Bongani would ask.

"I can get a pair of Nikes for 150."

"Okay, instead of you giving us 140, we'll give you 10, and you get us a pair of Nikes with your discount." [51]

Now it gets even better because the guy owns now a DVD player and has an extra 10 rands in his pockets. He brings the Nike shoes a few days later, which Trevor and Bongani can sell in a white neighborhood for 200 rands. So, with just 60 rands, in this case, they made 200 rands. If the guy comes back with a pair of Nike shoes, the sacred rule is not to ask where they are from, as they can be stolen or they can be bought using the staff discount. Their core activity shifted from pirate CDs and DJ-ing to the money-lending business, which was profitable. People would rather come to them for a short-term loan, instead of going to a dangerous gangster, who would hurt them if they failed to pay. First of all, this wasn't their style, and secondly, they weren't capable of such terrible acts.

Moms struggling to buy food to feed their families would come to them, knowing that nobody would have their legs broken if they failed to pay the loan. In some cases, Bongani would make the craziest deals (especially when it came to moms with beautiful daughters), even Trevor couldn't believe where he got the ideas. Until the mom paid the loan, she couldn't keep them away from her house. They would drop by, have a small chat with her daughter; when the mom started to trust them they get invited to dinner and then the mom would even agree to let the daughter go with them to a party with the condition that the girl will be safely returned home. Then, Bongani worked some deals with different guys.

"Hey, let's make a deal. We'll bring the girl to your party, and you get to hang out with her. How much can you give us?"

"I don't have money," he'd say, "but I have some cases of beer."

"Okay, so tonight we're going to this party. You give us two cases of beer for the party."

"Cool." [52]

They would go with the girl to the party; the guy would get to hang out with her. Bongani and Trevor would then receive the beers and make some money by selling them. In some cases, they would also write off the debt to the mother, as a sign of gratitude. They were the kind lenders, unlike the ruthless gangsters or the big banks.

Trevor and Bongani would receive plenty of money in the form of interest. At the peak of their operation, they had around 10,000 rands in cash and stocks of DVD players, other electronic goods, or Jordans to sell. In terms of cost, they had to buy blank CDs, buy food, and hire mini-busses to go to different DJ gigs. Using spreadsheets was something that Trevor learned from his mother. He used this system to keep track of loans, so they had sheets with names of persons they lent money to, the amount of money owed, or when they paid or didn't pay.

Things were going in the same routine in the hood, everyday hustling, everyday trying to make money out of money. It already passed two years since graduation from Sandringham High-School, and Trevor's dream of becoming a computer programmer slowly faded away, because no matter how much money they would make out of interest and selling stuff, the money would not be enough to enroll for the university. He later realized that as soon as things are going well for you in the hood, that's the perfect time to get out of there. If not, the hood would drag you back in and it's becoming a place that you can't get out of it because you depend on the hood, and you probably think that you can't become successful outside of the hood.

Chapter 8:
Things are Falling Apart

Downfall

Soon the CD copying business was coming to an end because Trevor lost all his music, thousands and thousands of tracks. The crew was at a DJ gig in Lombardy East, a very nice neighborhood for black middle-class people. Somebody made a complaint about the noise, and the police busted in to stop the party. In South Africa, the police are always equipped with riot control gear when having an intervention in a black neighborhood, so they looked like the American SWAT troops. They were looking for the source of music, and this led to Trevor and his computer. He was threatened with an assault rifle and was asked to shut down the music. The slow Windows 95 operating system from the PC was not very helpful in this case, as it took forever to close programs and shut down the computer. The hard drive was already damaged a bit, and he didn't want to cut the power and possibly destroy the hard drive. The policeman didn't have the patience for all of this and didn't understand that Trevor had to close all the programs. He didn't know too much about computers, so he shot the monitor, but the music continued to play. Everyone heard the gunshot and started to run out like crazy, Trevor pulled the power cord to shut the whole tower down and watched the police spraying tear gas into the crowd. The hard drive was destroyed, and Trevor lost all his music. Hours and hours of hard work and dedication of downloading tracks and mixing them were just lost. His CD copying and DJ days were over, so now the crew had to concentrate on money lending. Although they tried to keep the money flow coming, they couldn't keep up with the loss of all the music.

Soon they were going into their savings until that were also gone.

It looked like luck had forsaken the crew from Alexandra. They were invited to a dance competition in Soweto, and this was the perfect opportunity for Hitler to shine again. His competitor from Soweto, Hector, was one of the best dancers in South Africa. There was always a huge rivalry between Soweto and Alexandra, so now the guys had to represent their hood against the crew from Soweto. Hitler lost against Hector, G got them all in trouble when he was caught kissing one of their girls, and on top of that, the mini-bus was pulled over by the police on their way back to Alexandra. They were probably looking for some bribe because they framed them, placing a gun in the mini-bus.

"We've found a gun," he said. "Whose gun is it?"

We all shrugged.

"We don't know," we said.

"Nope, somebody knows. It's somebody's gun."

"Officer, we really don't know," Bongani said.

He slapped Bongani hard across the face.

"You're bullshitting me!"

Then he went down the line, slapping each of us across the face, berating us about the gun. We couldn't do anything but stand there and take it.

"You guys are trash," the cop said. "Where are you from?"

"Alex."

"Ohhhhh, okay, I see. Dogs from Alex. You come here, and you rob people, and you rape women, and you hijack cars. Bunch of fucking hoodlums."

"No, we're dancers. We don't know—"

"I don't care. You're all going to jail until we figure out whose gun this is." [53]

At one point they got to the point, trying to find a solution for this situation. They were looking for a bribe, but nobody from the crew had any money on them, so they ended up in jail. It was a public mini-bus, but only they were arrested for supposedly having a gun with them. At the police station, they were all thrown in a cell and then they took them one by one for interrogation. They spent the night and the next day in jail until Trevor called a friend who could borrow some money from his dad to bail them out. They were eventually bailed out, but there was no paperwork, nothing to mention that the amount was paid for bail, not for a bribe. The dream of making money from the hood was over, and the guys never recovered after this incident they had with the police. Surviving the hood was getting more difficult than ever, and for everyone in their situations there can only be two options: to get a job at McDonald's to flip burgers, or to continue what they were doing and rise again, following the rules of the hood. Trevor chose to be part of that world, although he wasn't from that world. So he was some impostor, but unlike the others, he could escape from the hood.

Jail

Being arrested in the hood was just something natural, as you had to be a saint over there not to be arrested. Even Bongani got arrested, which left Trevor very sad. His best friend, his "partner in crime," was not arrested, and he somehow had to make money without Bongani. Trevor's mom hated the hood; she didn't want to live in such an environment and didn't want Trevor to waste his time over there. She didn't like his friends either, and whenever they were stopping by, she didn't want them coming in. It's not like she hated them, but she most likely hated the place where they were coming from. Patricia always thought very highly of her nephew Mlungisi, who was attending the university and wanted Trevor to spend more time with him. She always thought that the hood was not a suitable environment for her son, as it would hold him down. The university is a different environment which would encourage him to become better and make something of himself.

"What's the difference if I'm at university or I'm in the hood?" I'd say. "It's not like I'm going to university."

"Yes, but the pressure of the university is going to get you. I know you.

79

You won't sit by and watch these guys become better than you. If you're in an environment that is positive and progressive, you too will become that. I keep telling you to change your life, and you don't. One day you're going to get arrested, and when you do, don't call me. I'll tell the police to lock you up to teach you a lesson." [54]

Things were not going very well for Trevor with Bongani being in prison, as he had to come up with different plan to keep the business running, buying stuff and selling them back. One day, Trevor noticed an advertisement in a newspaper. The ad was about a clearance sale for mobile phones at a shop. He was determined to buy a lot of phones and sell them back as he still had some of Bongani's connections. His stepfather had a lot of junk cars, most of them which weren't even street legal. He stole cars since he was 14, and he always thought he was test driving them to check if Abel repaired them correctly. His stepfather didn't find this very funny, but he never punished him—Patricia was doing that. This time Trevor was determined to get the phones and sell them at a good price, and nothing could stand in his way. There were some old registration plates in the garage which he could use on the car he was trying to use. He would use the same red Mazda he drove at the matric dance. He wasn't thinking of any possible consequences, and he was more afraid of the reactions his parents would have, than being stopped by the police.

He drove to the shop to buy the mobile phone, but he never made it over there. Trevor was pulled over by the police, and soon the police discovered there was something wrong with the registration plates. The police officer ran a check on the registration plates, and they didn't match the car. Without any hesitation, the cop arrested Trevor under the suspicion of driving a stolen car. At the police station, the cop also ran a check on the car, which also didn't have certain ownership. They had all the elements to believe that Trevor has stolen that car and tried to put different registration plates on it.

Trevor didn't have any choice but to spend the night in jail, as he was picked up late in the afternoon by the officer and couldn't have a bail hearing that day. Bail hearings always work in favor of the convicted, if he could get a dedicated lawyer who could take care of the case very seriously.

They were successful in convincing the judge to pardon the convicted one in exchange for bail. Trevor didn't have any money for a proper lawyer, and if he wanted to get the bail hearing, most likely he would end up with a state attorney who couldn't care less about him and normally didn't even bother to check his file. Also, because he was picked up so late by the police, he missed the bail hearing for the day, so he had to spend the night in jail. He was also advised by one of the police officers not to consider the bail hearing, as it wouldn't work in his favor with a state attorney. He had to right to stay in that jail for as long as he wanted. Just before lights off, an officer came to him to get his belt, shoelaces (so he didn't hang himself) and wallet.

Trevor encouraged himself, being convinced that this was not that bad and he could make it in there. There was a huge difference between prison and jail. The prison was hell on Earth, where prisoners were being raped, hurt, or even killed. The jail was just a joke compared to the prison, as there were always cops walking by and everyone in there was under supervision so that nothing could go wrong. There was a well-known fact in South Africa that the most ruthless criminals and murderers were the colored gang members. So there he was, a colored individual standing in jail. He decided to have fun and make the most out of this experience, so play the role of a crazy and violent colored criminal. He also noticed that most of his cellmates were in there for minor offenses like drunk driving, minor theft, or domestic abuse. They didn't know what real gangster was like. Trevor started to impersonate the violent colored gang member stereotype, to impose himself as the only badass in the cell. He used a thick colored accent to say something in a broken Afrikaans language, to strike fear in the hearts of his cellmates. He was just like a white guy, with a slightly darker skin trying to act like a Mexican gang member, acting all "loco."

No one said a word to each other in the cell; everyone was posing as being on guard, not saying anything, because after all, that wasn't a support group. There weren't any dangerous criminals in that cell, but still, nobody was saying a word. Trevor thought he could do this, as the food in jail was above his expectations. He had peanut butter sandwiches for breakfast, chicken and rice for lunch and a hot tea, which was drinkable boiled water with a slight taste of tea. Trevor was enjoying his stay in prison, as he didn't have any stress, no chores to do, no constant struggle to make money, no nagging from anyone, it was great for him. He could stay in there forever, as he was scared of the beating that would be waiting for him at home. He was planning to stay over there for a few years and then go back to his family pretending he was kidnapped, and Patricia would be super thrilled to see him again.

His mood changed in the third week when the police officers brought in the biggest guy Trevor had ever seen. He looked like a black Hulk, capable of killing anyone in the cell. The cop was trying to interrogate the Hulk, he was speaking Zulu, but the guy didn't understand. He was speaking Tsonga, a rare language in South Africa, just like Pedi (the language spoken by Trevor's matric dance date – Babiki). Trevor learned this language from his stepfather, Abel, who was Tsonga. Since the cop was not able to communicate with the huge black guy, Trevor stepped in and translated their discussion, sorting everything out. Trevor spoke in the native language of the guy and discovered that the Hulk was not, in fact, a raging monster, but was a sweet and kind person. He was locked for stealing PlayStation games, as he was currently unemployed and wanted to send some money to his family back home. When he noticed how much those games were, he wanted to steal them and then sell them to make a lot of money. Trevor understood Hulk's point of view, as he was very familiar with the world of pirated CDs, even for video games. Stolen video games had no value because it was way too risky, and it was cheaper to copy them. Trevor found out his story and felt pity for him, as he was now in jail, not understanding English at all, and when he would have the bail hearing everyone would assume the worst of him, and he wouldn't have any chance to walk out of that hearing room a free man.

When Trevor had his hearing, he was taken to the courtroom in handcuffs. The courtroom didn't only host hearings for people coming from jail; they also had hearings for those from prison who were waiting for trials for weeks or months. There was a cell where they put all of them in together, jail and prison, so Trevor was stuck in that cell with really dangerous and violent gang members. He had to pick a side again, just like he did in school, but this time he had to make a very inspired decision and choose the less dangerous group. On one side there was the colored group, the ruthless murderers that everybody was so afraid of. He couldn't do the badass act now, not in there and not with them because they could easily discover that Trevor was an impostor. This time, Trevor chose white for obvious reasons (they were the least dangerous group in there). In the white corner, there were mostly middle-aged guys convicted of fraud or money laundering. It was safe for him to stay with the white guys, but he was also lucky to stay in there just for about an hour. He was called in the hearing room, and as he was leaving the cell, a white guy approached him. "Make sure you don't come back down here," he said. "Cry in front of the judge; do whatever you have to do. If you go up and get sent back down here, your life will never be the same." [55]

Trevor's cousin Mlungisi was in the hearing room, ready to bail him out, everything went fine, and Trevor was released. His cousin drove Trevor back home to meet with his mom and he noticed Patricia's look. It wasn't anger; it was a severe disappointment, as she was deeply hurt. Probably Trevor would have preferred a severe beating instead of seeing that look on her mother's face. She knew where Trevor was; she knew what he had done. As Trevor was thinking of schemes in prison how to tell the story, the proof of his crime was undeniable. The red Mazda was missing from the driveway. This is how Trevor found out that the money for his bail was, in fact, the money his mother sent through his cousin Mlungisi. After a week in jail, he thought he was so cool, but his mom knew everything the whole time.

"I know you see me as some crazy old bitch nagging at you," she said, "but you forget the reason I ride you so hard and give you so much shit is because I love you—everything I have ever done I've done from a place of love. If I don't punish you, the world will punish you even worse. The world doesn't love you. If the police get you, the police don't love you. When I beat you, I'm trying to save you. When they beat you, they're trying to kill you." [56]

Chapter 9:
Abel

A bel was the guy Patricia was dating when Trevor was about six years old. From Trevor's birth, until she started dating Abel, she was a single and independent mother, trying to offer a disciplinary education to little Trevor. Patricia's second-hand car was the reason they met, as the car was breaking down frequently. Abel was a very skilled mechanic, who came to like Patricia, as she was a faithful customer. He was working for Mighty Mechanics, a garage in the Yeoville neighborhood, very close to Robert's house. When they started dating, Trevor was too young to realize what was happening, but he does remember that Patricia was stopping by the garage, even though the Volkswagen was not broken at that time. They had chemistry, but Patricia didn't anticipate the monster that he would become. She liked him, and they had cute nicknames for each other. He called her Mbuyi, short for Mbuyiselo, and she would call him Abie. Trevor liked him at the beginning, as he was the helpful kind of guy who would help anyone in distress. He never tried to be Trevor's dad, and that's what he appreciated of him. Abie was always acting like the cool older brother, the one you can count on when you were getting into trouble.

Abel was very passionate about cars and mechanics. So passionate that he transformed the garage where he was fixing cars into a living space, where Patricia and Trevor would sometimes sleep over, as it was very close to her work and also close enough to Trevor's fancy Catholic School. At the beginning of the relationship he had with Patricia, an incident marked the future development of the relationship. Trevor burnt down the house of the white family, and they asked Abel to pack his stuff and move. From that point, he was living with them in Eden Park. Abel would constantly have fights with Patricia saying "Your son burnt down my life." Patricia and Trevor would soon discover the hidden side of Abel, his violent side, as his bad temper got the most of him. Abel was his English name, but his Tsonga name was Ngisaveni, which meant "Be afraid." They were legally married for about four or five years, but after that, they divorced, but they continue to live together as a family. With the Mulberry tree incident, Abel against lost his temper and severely beat a 12-year-old child who was bullying Trevor. Whenever he lost his temper, he simply had the "devil eyes," which was a good sign just to stay away from him. Before dating Patricia, Abel was smoking weed, but during his relationship with her, he switched to alcohol. When he was drunk, there was no reasoning with him, as he was not thinking straight, and he would be abusive and violent. However, not only alcohol turned him into a monster. It was his uncontrolled anger and bad temper which transformed him into a raging beast. Patricia was the victim of his violence, and she would repeatedly go to the police station to file complaints against him. The police never intervened for domestic abuse, as they always considered this is a problem which had to be sorted out in the family and shouldn't be police business. Although he was abusive to Patricia and then as soon as Trevor grew up, was also abusive towards him and violent also, Patricia still gave him two sons: Andrew and Isaac. Naturally, it wasn't a happy marriage, as she would take refuge in going to church, while he would drink too much. Abel was a great mechanic, but he wasn't good at doing business. Patricia even loved him enough to sell the house she had and invest all the money into his business, the Mighty Mechanics garage. He eventually had to close the garage, as the business was in debt and could no longer continue. This was the point when everything got even worse. The violence and abuse would be something frequent until Patricia eventually left him, moved to a different location, and lived with someone else. But Abel didn't want to let go and even tried to kill her, but he didn't succeed. By the time Trevor was already a successful comedian, he received a call from his brother, Andrew, when he was at the hospital. This is how he found out what happened. Abel came by Patricia's home determined to kill her, but first, he aimed the gun at Andrew, but like the great mother that she is, Patricia put herself between the gun and her son. She got shot in the leg, then in her behind, but also she was shot in the head. Trevor came immediately to the hospital and burst into tears when he saw his mother's condition. It was a miracle that she didn't die, as the bullet went through the back of her head and came out from her face. The doctors did their best, and they were able to save her. It looked like all the visits to church and the fact that she was a religious fanatic had finally paid off.

His mom eventually got well and was sent home, but Abel only spent one year in prison for attempted murder. He threatened to kill Trevor as well, so Trevor had to leave South Africa for the US and pursue his television career over there.

Closing Thoughts

S tand-up comedy is better when the stories told on stage are from the comedian's experience. Being raised in a racist regime and experiencing all kind of hard situations, Trevor learned how to get the most out of any experience he had. Starting from the early childhood days, when he could have been considered the "colored" "Dennis the Menace," until his late teenage days when he was still getting in trouble, Trevor has a lot of funny stories to tell. He also has a very funny way of telling the stories and emphasize the ridicule of any experience. He was the naughty but also a friendly kid, who could always make you laugh. Being a polyglot (he speaks plenty of languages like English, Afrikaans, Xhosa, Zulu, Tsonga, Sotho) he was one of the few who could easily blend in every social group, as he was familiar with white kids or black kids. The only kids who openly hated him were ironically his kind, the "colored." Only his mother's disappointment after spending time in jail finally made him grow up and become a man. That was the starting point of his career, as he soon after that became a comedian and shared his stories with the rest of the world.

He also started his TV and radio career, as he was starting to host shows across South Africa and the UK. Soon he started to become famous also in the US, after his performance on *Gabriel Iglesias Presents Stand – Up Revolution*. After this representation, he had his very own comedy specials, which aired on American television. This is how the American people found out more details regarding him and about the monstrous political regime called apartheid. At the moment, he is hosting the very popular TV show on Comedy Central called, *The Daily Show*. The best stand-up comedy comes from personal experiences, and Trevor has plenty of experiences to tell. His comedic influences were black American comedians like Richard Pryor, Bill Cosby, Eddie Murphy, Chris Rock, and Dave Chappelle. A big influence on his life was also made by the comedian Jon Stewart, who saw in him his worthy successor for *The Daily Show*.

His reputation increased a lot after being appointed the host for *The Daily Show*. But even before having this honor, he received several awards in South Africa and also North America. Some of the awards would be Best Host, Favorite African Star, and many others. His autobiography "Born a Crime" was the #1 New York Times Bestseller, and at the moment there is also a project of making a movie based on this book, with Lupita Nyong'o, starring as Trevor's mom, Patricia. He is also known for his funny tweets and comments regarding President Donald Trump.

Bibliography

T. Noah (2016), Born a Crime, New York, Spiegel & Grau

[1] T. Noah (2016), Born a Crime, p. 48, New York, Spiegel & Grau

[2] T. Noah (2016), Born a Crime, p. 50, New York, Spiegel & Grau

[3] T. Noah (2016), Born a Crime, p. 51, New York, Spiegel & Grau

[4] T. Noah (2016), Born a Crime, p. 51, New York, Spiegel & Grau

[5] T. Noah (2016), Born a Crime, p. 51, New York, Spiegel & Grau

[6] T. Noah (2016), Born a Crime, p. 51, New York, Spiegel & Grau

[7] T. Noah (2016), Born a Crime, p. 52, New York, Spiegel & Grau

[8] T. Noah (2016), Born a Crime, p. 53, New York, Spiegel & Grau

[9] T. Noah (2016), Born a Crime, p. 53, New York, Spiegel & Grau

[10] T. Noah (2016), Born a Crime, p. 53, New York, Spiegel & Grau

[11] T. Noah (2016), Born a Crime, p. 54, New York, Spiegel & Grau

[12] T. Noah (2016), Born a Crime, p. 54, New York, Spiegel & Grau

[13] T. Noah (2016), Born a Crime, p. 54, New York, Spiegel & Grau

[14] T. Noah (2016), Born a Crime, p. 54, New York, Spiegel & Grau

[15] T. Noah (2016), Born a Crime, p. 55, New York, Spiegel & Grau

[16] T. Noah (2016), Born a Crime, p. 55, New York, Spiegel & Grau

[17] T. Noah (2016), Born a Crime, p. 69, New York, Spiegel & Grau

[18] T. Noah (2016), Born a Crime, p. 69, New York, Spiegel & Grau

[19] T. Noah (2016), Born a Crime, p. 69, New York, Spiegel & Grau

[20] T. Noah (2016), Born a Crime, p. 69, New York, Spiegel & Grau

[21] T. Noah (2016), Born a Crime, p. 71, New York, Spiegel & Grau

[22] Noah (2016), Born a Crime, p. 72, New York, Spiegel & Grau

[23] T. Noah (2016), Born a Crime, p. 73, New York, Spiegel & Grau

[24] T. Noah (2016), Born a Crime, p. 77, New York, Spiegel & Grau

[25] T. Noah (2016), Born a Crime, p. 77, New York, Spiegel & Grau

[26] T. Noah (2016), Born a Crime, p. 77, New York, Spiegel & Grau

[27] T. Noah (2016), Born a Crime, p. 78, New York, Spiegel & Grau

[28] T. Noah (2016), Born a Crime, p. 78, New York, Spiegel & Grau

[29] T. Noah (2016), Born a Crime, p. 78, New York, Spiegel & Grau

[30] T. Noah (2016), Born a Crime, p. 78, New York, Spiegel & Grau

[31] T. Noah (2016), Born a Crime, p. 88, New York, Spiegel & Grau

[32] T. Noah (2016), Born a Crime, p. 98, New York, Spiegel & Grau

[33] T. Noah (2016), Born a Crime, p. 99, New York, Spiegel & Grau

[34] T. Noah (2016), Born a Crime, p. 100, New York, Spiegel & Grau

[35] T. Noah (2016), Born a Crime, p. 101, New York, Spiegel & Grau

[36] T. Noah (2016), Born a Crime, p. 103, New York, Spiegel & Grau

[37] T. Noah (2016), Born a Crime, p. 104, New York, Spiegel & Grau

[38] T. Noah (2016), Born a Crime, p. 105, New York, Spiegel & Grau

[39] T. Noah (2016), Born a Crime, p. 110, New York, Spiegel & Grau

[40] T. Noah (2016), Born a Crime, p. 111, New York, Spiegel & Grau

[41] T. Noah (2016), Born a Crime, p. 111, New York, Spiegel & Grau

[42] T. Noah (2016), Born a Crime, p. 112, New York, Spiegel & Grau

[43] T. Noah (2016), Born a Crime, p. 113, New York, Spiegel & Grau

[44] T. Noah (2016), Born a Crime, p. 115-116, New York, Spiegel & Grau

[45] T. Noah (2016), Born a Crime, p. 116-117, New York, Spiegel & Grau

[46] T. Noah (2016), Born a Crime, p. 117, New York, Spiegel & Grau

[47] T. Noah (2016), Born a Crime, p. 117, New York, Spiegel & Grau

[48] T. Noah (2016), Born a Crime, p. 117, New York, Spiegel & Grau

[49] T. Noah (2016), Born a Crime, p. 122, New York, Spiegel & Grau

[50] T. Noah (2016), Born a Crime, p. 123, New York, Spiegel & Grau

[51] T. Noah (2016), Born a Crime, p. 124, New York, Spiegel & Grau

[52] T. Noah (2016), Born a Crime, p. 126, New York, Spiegel & Grau

[53] T. Noah (2016), Born a Crime, p. 130, New York, Spiegel & Grau

[54] T. Noah (2016), Born a Crime, p. 133, New York, Spiegel & Grau

[55] T. Noah (2016), Born a Crime, p. 141, New York, Spiegel & Grau

[56] T. Noah (2016), Born a Crime, p. 142, New York, Spiegel & Grau

Made in the USA
Las Vegas, NV
08 September 2022

54895363R00059